And the Word Increased

And the Word Increased

A Study of the Progress of the Gospel in the Days of Paul

J. H. Bavinck

trans. Harry Van Dyke

WORDBRIDGE PUBLISHING
Aalten, the Netherlands
www.wordbridge.net
info@wordbridge.net

Original Dutch edition: *Alzoo wies het Woord. Een studie over den voortgang van het evangelie in de dagen van Paulus.* Baarn: Bosch & Keuning, 1942, reprinted 1960.

ISBN 978-90-836612-0-9

COVER AND TITLE PAGE ILLUSTRATION: "St. Paul Preaching in Athens" by Raphael (1515). This photographic reproduction is in the public domain.

Table of Contents

Translator's Notes vii
Author's Introduction ix
1. In the Line of Fire 1
    Impeding forces 2
    The circumcision question: church and nation 8
    The circumcision question: law and gospel 12
    Missions without missionaries 13
2. Paul and the Itinerant Preachers 21
    The background of Paul's activity 21
    The style of the work 28
        (i) increasing concentration 29
        (ii) based on principle 32
        (iii) maintaining continuity 33
        (iv) repeated recruitment of fresh human resources 34
    Paul and his aides 36
    Summary 41
3. The World of Paul's Struggles 43
    The demise of the national religions 43
    The new world 47
    Intellectual-spiritual movements 51
        Cosmopolitanism 51
        Liberalism 54
        Moralism 56
        Syncretism 56
        Mysticism 59
    Twilight 63

MAPS OF PAUL'S MISSIONARY TRAVELS 68

4. Preaching the Gospel on the Mission Field 71
    What Paul himself says about it 71
    Preaching the gospel in Lystra 76
    Preaching before the philosophers of Athens 80
    Some short passages 83
    Why does Paul preach in this way? 85
5. The Mystery of Mars Hill 91
    Multiple opinions 91
    A literary approach 95
    Paul's speech in more recent theology 100

Why so gentle? ... 101
Gospel and philosophy ... 103
Concluding observations ... 110
Summary ... 113
6. The Young Church in a Pagan World ... 115
Church and world ... 115
Shaping congregational life ... 118
The Church and social and political relations ... 123
The Church and her relation to her pagan surroundings ... 125
Questions about faith ... 128
7. The Church on the Offensive ... 133
A journey of centuries ... 133
A task for everybody ... 135
The world then and our world now ... 138
How then shall we preach? ... 139
Appendix ... 143
In Memoriam Dr. H. A. van Andel ... 143
Index of Scripture References ... 147
Index of Authors Cited ... 151
Index of Names ... 153
Index of Subjects ... 155

Translator's Notes

Among the many writings of J. H. Bavinck we are fortunate to have this insightful study of Paul's missionary work as recorded in the Book of Acts and reflected in the Pauline epistles. In 1941, when he wrote this book, Johan Herman Bavinck (1895–1964) had served for seventeen years as a missionary pastor and teacher on the island of Java. In the quarter century that followed, he would develop into an influential missiologist teaching at Reformed theological faculties in Kampen and Amsterdam, where he also composed his well-known *Inleiding in de Zendingswetenschap.*[1]

The author's target readership for the present modest-sized book appears to be the general reader interested in foreign missions and homeland evangelism. At the same time, the book comes across as the first draft of a handbook on "best practices" in the mission field. The original book was illustrated with twenty-two photographs of sculptures from antiquity, Greco-Roman temples, paintings of St. Paul, and Raphael's mural "The School of Athens."[2] A semi-popular book perhaps, but its pages speak of unquestionable erudition and persuasive psychological insights. Of particular interest is its combination of historical analysis and present-day relevance. The reader pricks up his ears whenever Bavinck describes a custom or a school of thought in the world of the Early Church, or explains a cultural feature in Paul's days, and then adds: "and it is still that way on the mission field today." Today, the ordinary church member may wonder if that is still true after eighty years of decolonization, globalism, and the internet, but students of Bavinck who are able to judge assure us that his insights are as relevant today as ever.[3] In an Appendix I have reproduced an *In Memoriam* which Bavinck wrote about a former mentor and colleague and in

[1] Kampen: Kok, 1954. Eng. trans. by David H. Freeman, *Introduction to the Science of Missions* (Philadelphia: Presbyterian and Reformed Pub. Co., 1960).

[2] These illustrations formed part of the semipopular character of the book. In this translation, only Raphael's painting of Paul on Mars Hill is retained.

[3] See comments by missiologists Jo Verkuyl and Roger Greenway, quoted in Paul Jan Visser, *Heart for the Gospel, Heart for the World: The Life and Thought of a Reformed Pioneer Missiologist Johan Herman Bavinck, 1895–1964* (Eugene, OR: Wipf and Stock, 2003), pp. viii, x.

which he gives us a glimpse of what he most admired in the work of this missionary.

If I may be allowed a note of more than just historical interest: Bavinck always stressed the claim of the gospel on the whole of life. Even as he wrote this book his daughter and his two sons got involved in the Resistance movement against the godless regime of national socialism by helping Jewish persons in hiding with safe hiding addresses, stolen ration cards, and forged IDs, and by distributing contraband newsletters. All three survived the war, the younger son only after a year's stay in a German concentration camp.

My translation stays as close as possible, of course, to the original, but it does not hesitate at times to resort to dynamic equivalents. The hardest pages were the ones that read like poetry. For the title of his book Bavinck took the words from Acts 19:20. For special terminology I have consulted the author's *Introduction to the Science of Missions* as well as *The J. H. Bavinck Reader*[4] and the study mentioned in note 3. Scripture citations are taken from the English Standard Version.

Nienke Wolters Van Dyke read through the first draft and offered valuable suggestions. Al Wolters did the same with the second draft and also helped with the Greek. Bibliographic references in the footnotes have been brought up to contemporary scholarly standards. My annotation appears in square brackets.

The author did not dedicate his book to anyone in particular. This translation I dedicate to Al Wolters, who first drew my attention to this inspiring book sixty years ago, during our graduate study days at the Free University, where Bavinck had taught.

Hamilton, Ontario
Fall 2025

Harry Van Dyke, D.Litt.
Redeemer University

[4] John Bolt, et al., eds., *The J. H. Bavinck Reader* (Grand Rapids, MI: Baker, 2013).

Author's Introduction

One of the most hopeful signs that fill us with great joy in these depressing times is the fact that the Church realizes more keenly than ever before that she must be on the attack. We are not thinking now of a specific church or denomination but of the World Church as a whole, as it toils and moils in our turbulent days. The Church understands that she is called to proclaim the gospel of Jesus Christ in the world in which she lives and which surrounds her on all sides.

This realization did not arise suddenly but developed gradually with growing certainty. As early as the 18th century, the Church of modern times began to feel uneasy about unfinished business, about her calling to go out to distant lands and bring the message of salvation to people. It was then that the great missionary movement was born that continues heroically to this day. When, soon thereafter, unbelief began to gain ground throughout Europe and many people grew estranged from faith in God, the Church began to sense keenly that proclaiming the gospel was required also on the home front. After all, the Lord's command had first mentioned going to Jerusalem and only thereafter going "*to the end of the earth*" (Acts 1:8). From that day forward, as the Church entered the 19th century, she embarked upon proclaiming the Word more intensely than ever before in her own environment.

And so we have been preaching the Word that we acknowledge to be the Word of life. It cannot be denied, however, that we are anything but skilled at it. We feel out of our element. We don't know where to begin and where to end. At times we feel small and intimidated. We have to contend with the irrepressible urge to crawl back within the safe walls of our own little world. It takes a good deal of courage and perseverance to stay on the offensive, even when defense seems most called for.

For this reason it can be very important for us to carefully study by what strategy the Church of the first century went on the offensive. More than former generations, we are fascinated by what the apostles did in obedient response to the mandate of their Sender. And among the apostles the one that rises most prominently before our eyes is the one who called himself "*a preacher, and an apostle, and a teacher of the Gentiles*" (2 Tim. 1:11 KJV). We are automatically drawn to Paul—to the apostle who in word and deed proved himself a good instrument in the hands of Him who was willing to use him for this great work.

The purpose of the present volume is to sketch the work of this apostle in his missionary activity. Our aim will not be to consider all kinds of details about his missionary journeys; we are not going to follow him on all his treks through Asia Minor and Greece. Rather, we want to tap the secret of this life, a life that went on the offensive. God's grace gave him strength in the most anxious moments and enabled him to labour more abundantly than all the other apostles (1 Cor. 15:10).

Living many centuries later, we look with envy at Paul's work and cannot shake the feeling that God has something grand to tell us through Paul's life. We are not apostles; we cannot place ourselves alongside him; we cannot compare our life and work to Paul's. But prayerful study of what God accomplished through his labours can strengthen and inspire us for the task that awaits us.

1. In the Line of Fire

A glow of joy and enthusiasm lies over the first century of the history of the Christian Church. The young church struggled like a tiny army that was beset in the rear by the grim hostility of the Jewish people and its leaders, while her front line was continually hard pressed by the enormous political, cultural, and philosophical powers of a pagan world. She was the butt of vile gossip and the target of a whole arsenal of philosophical arguments about the preposterous nature of the gospel. As if that was not enough, her flanks were continually attacked by heretical schools that aspired to mix the gospel of Jesus Christ with all kinds of Jewish and pagan notions. This little army had to find its own way, valiantly and fearlessly. It did not flinch when cursed and condemned. In the most critical times it remained faithful to the Captain of their salvation and the Author and Finisher of their faith. Owing to the unyielding force with which it carried on the struggle, it gained ground step by step, even though it had to pay for every inch with the blood of its martyrs. Without swords or daggers, it penetrated to within the walls of the imperial palace, and it knocked on the door of the world for as long as it took to gain admittance.

Small wonder that later centuries looked back with a kind of nostalgia on that first period of the Church's history, when believers radiated confidence that God could do incredible things through the followers of Christ. The world at that time did not look like a deadweight that could no longer be moved. It was considered worth the trouble to assail the world, not give it a moment's rest, and pursue it into the remotest hide-outs. Boundless expectations filled the hearts of all who in those days rallied behind Jesus Christ as the only Lord and Saviour. We, who have so many more centuries behind us, feel tired and powerless when we compare ourselves with those early Christians and their brave hopes and bold actions. We too are nostalgic about those first days. We think back of that era with respect and envy, a time when the Church was still on the offensive, when the faith was alive and thrived, "in spite of dungeon, fire and sword."

But why do we feel so strongly about these things today? I think it's because the Church is becoming increasingly aware that she is surrounded by a world in which all kinds of hostile powers are turning against her. She is beginning to realize something of the threat that hangs over her head, of the tremendous struggle she will have to wage. The great cities of our world are increasingly estranged from any faith in God and Jesus Christ. New ideas and new expectations captivate the hearts of millions of people. No wonder that we today realize more powerfully than ever before what a great treasure had been entrusted to the Early Church.

But how was it possible that those small circles of believers in so short a time achieved such astounding victories? How did they organize their campaign? Along what lines did they penetrate the camp of their adversaries? Were they not held back by the inertia that immediately paralyzes us whenever we, in our day, mount an action? Were they never in danger of being overcome by loss of heart or the irresistible desire to take shelter in the safety of the trenches? When they walked the streets of the urban centers of their day, did they not feel a sense of futility about preaching the gospel there? Were the people of those days different from people today? Was the opposition less vehement? Were the obstacles less intimidating?

All these questions deserve our closest attention. Studying church history does not just mean that we research all kinds of interesting events. It asks much more from us. We too are people who believe in Jesus Christ, and we have our place in the history of the Church. We too live in a world of unbelief and enmity. We may be deeply moved as we pore over those old documents, and tears may well up in our eyes as we read how those first Christians stood in the line of fire; but sooner or later we must draw the consequences of this knowledge and ask what this means for us. How are we to respond? How can some of that same power fill our hearts again? That is the question on the lips of us all. That is the question we take with us as we set out to study the initial expansion of the Church of Christ. We want to see that Church in her assault on the strongholds of paganism.

Impeding forces

It has sometimes been pointed out that Luke, as he composed his book on the Acts of the Apostles, was guided by the motivation to show how missionary activity under divine guidance grew organically out of the first churches. And indeed, in Luke's account this missionary activity unfolds gradually in concentric circles: the apostles first preach to Jews who used to live elsewhere; they then turn to Samaritans, then to proselytes, followed by a pagan centurion being added to the church; and finally, there are Gentile Christian churches.[5] We dare not say whether this was indeed Luke's deliberate composition. But in any event, it is a fact that his book demonstrates how slowly and calmly the work among the Gentiles unfolded.

At the same time, we should point out that Luke also clearly exposes the different factors that impeded the missionary activity. One might be justified to characterize the first period of church history with these words: *How God pushed his sluggish and reluctant church to take up her mission.*

The first impediment appears shortly after the Ascension. As Jesus Christ disappears before their eyes, the apostles are standing on the Mount of Olives, looking up to heaven. There is something of longing in their gaze, of being unable to part with one who had become so dear to them. Now then, that same longing is part of the entire Church during her first period. But what the angels then say to the apostles immediately transposes their longing into an active waiting for the Lord's return. "*This Jesus, who was taken up from you into heaven, will come in the same way as you saw him go into heaven*" (Acts 1:11). From that point on, circles of believers have an eschatological orientation to the Second Coming. It is a focus that does not slacken or slow them down but rather stimulates them to the greatest exertions. It gives all that activity in the first century of the Church an element of hurry and haste, as if they constantly feel that the day of the consummation of the ages is at hand: *Maranatha!* Jesus is coming! All missionary activity by the Early Church is borne up by a hopeful anticipation of Christ's return.

After the Ascension we find the group of apostles in Jerusalem. They have gathered in some upper room, in the company of several women as well as the brothers of Jesus who apparently by then already had come to the faith. This circle expands. In the very next verse (Acts 1:15) we hear of 120 people. That is not yet an expansion—more a question of rallying. These people sense that as individuals in that great hostile world they will be trodden underfoot; they will need to be united and strongly focused if they are to survive.

Apparently, this is how all the followers of Jesus living in Jerusalem—and perhaps also a few from Galilee who were in Jerusalem at the time—came

---

[5] Johannes Weiss, *Das Urchristentum*, 2 vols. (Gottingen: Vandenhoeck and Ruprecht, 1917), p. 151.

together to form one circle. In that circle the apostles were the natural leaders because they had personally seen the Resurrected One, but even more so because they had been commissioned by the Lord himself. Their next act too was still not outreach. In one of their meetings they chose an apostle to take the place of Judas who had betrayed Jesus. Thus, before taking any action to reach out, the Church first busied herself with internal organization to firm up her inner strength. The call to action could not be issued until all impediments had first been removed within the Church herself.

Then followed a period of waiting, but not as a sign of fear or inaction. Rather, they were waiting in obedience to Christ's instructions. He had commanded them to wait for the promise of the Father (Acts 1:4). The Church was surrounded by the Jewish world with its bitter hatred of the Crucified One. It would have been folly to confront that world in a burst of reckless presumption without first having received the power born of the Holy Spirit that was to be poured out on them.

Acts chapter 2, one of the sunniest pages in the Bible, tells of what happened to the entire first church when the Spirit of Christ descended upon them. Their eyes began to shine, their tongues started to speak, their hearts overflowed with renewed confidence and fresh anticipation. The day of Pentecost was the day when the first signal for the attack was given, followed by great victories. The large number of believers gained on the day of Pentecost evidently belonged to various groups. These included countless Palestinian Jews, either from Jerusalem itself or from other parts of the Holy Land. Secondly, included among the new converts were many Hellenists, Greek-speaking ethnic Jews who had lived abroad for a long time and as a result had lost some of the characteristic features of Jewish society. In the third place we hear of *proselytes*, persons of pagan background who had embraced the Jewish religion and after being circumcised had been received into the Jewish community. Acts 2:8–11 tells of a host of Hellenists from all parts of the then known world, as well as many proselytes who heard the gospel for the first time on that great day. All these groups were represented in the 3,000 souls that were added that day (Acts 2:41). That this included proselytes is abundantly clear from the account about the election to office of a certain Nicolaus, a proselyte of Antioch (Acts 6:5).

Thus, the first expansion of the Christian church took place in Jerusalem. The opening chapters of the book of Acts relate virtually nothing about activity in other parts of Palestine, not even in Galilee where the Lord had preached so often. All activity is focused on Jerusalem. New conquests were made daily, despite persecution from the Sanhedrin. How that was done, and by what routes this expansion rolled out, we are not told. In Jerusalem, of course, there were numerous people who had personally seen Jesus and witnessed his actions. It need not surprise us that the bold preaching of the apostles left a profound impression on people. There were plenty of places to mount a soapbox. Acts chapter 3 describes an extensive sermon by Peter that he delivered within the temple walls. Next to the temple at the center of the city, various synagogues offered excellent opportunities for preaching the gospel. The painful question that so often hampers us in missions—where best to reach people—was easily solved in Jerusalem. Precisely because it had not yet come to a break between church and synagogue, there were opportunities for contact on all sides.

About the social position of the believers we hear very little. Acts 6:1 speaks of Hellenists, while 6:7 mentions specifically that a great company of the priests were obedient to the faith. There is reason to assume that after their conversion these priests continued their service in the temple, even though some may have felt they could no longer carry out their temple duties.[6] No doubt there were many poor people among them who were cared for by the deacons. Some would have been poor to begin with, but others were poor as a direct result of the hatred of their fellow countrymen whose targets they had now become. As well, we know that some of these early believers owned houses and landed property. In this way the church in Jerusalem gradually grew into a force to be reckoned with. Later, when waves of hostility toward Christians washed over Jerusalem, the prestige of the apostles was already strong enough that the authorities decided not to arrest them (Acts 8:1).

Meanwhile the risk increased that the Christian church might bind herself too closely to the Jewish religion. A growing rapprochement seems to have developed in Jerusalem between the believers and devout Jews. A slow process of Judaizing the church set in. In Acts 21:20 we read that the church of Jerusalem, which by then counted many thousands, was composed largely of zealots for the

---

[6] Adolph Harnack, *Die Mission und Ausbreitung des Christentums in den ersten drei Jahrhunderten*, 3rd rev. ed. (Leipzig: Hinrichs), I, 51n [Eng. trans. James Moffatt, *The Expansion of Christianity in the First Three Centuries*, 2 vols. (New York: Putnam's, 1904), I, 51 n. 2].

law. A wind of pharisaism began to waft through the circle of believers, and such a strong measure of accommodating the Jewish environment took place that people began to view the Church as a sect within Judaism (Acts 28:22). In other words, the expansion of the first church rather soon got stuck. It got stuck geographically, confined as it was to Jerusalem. It also got stuck spiritually, being sucked back into the Jewish atmosphere which kept her from reaching out. Throughout the entire first period of church history, Jerusalem acted as a brake on any efforts at outreach. It took special leadings of God to remind the Church of her calling to be the messenger of glad tidings to the ends of the earth.

There is something of divine irony in the fact that these "special leadings" began as a result of the murmuring of a couple of widows. These Hellenist widows were not at all complaining because the light of the gospel was not shining brightly enough, but they complained—understandably enough—because during the daily distribution of food they were sometimes overlooked. Luke relates how in response to this discontent new officers were elected with the task of service (*diakonia*) at table during the daily love feasts. These new office-bearers introduced fresh blood, as it were, into the leadership of the church. They all had Greek names, which seems to indicate that there were several Hellenists among them, people who were familiar with other countries. We cannot be sure about that, for Palestinian Jews also took Greek names sometimes, yet the whole context does seem to point in that direction. As mentioned earlier, one of these seven men, Nicolaus, was a proselyte from Antioch. Anyway, these new office-bearers eagerly took up the *diakonia* of waiting at tables, but they soon turned out to be ardent preachers of the gospel as well. As a result, "*the word of God continued to increase*" (Acts 6:7).

One of the new appointees, Stephen, threw himself with heart and soul into bringing the gospel to those Hellenists who hailed from North Africa and Asia Minor. He availed himself of the synagogues that were especially built in Jerusalem for these expatriates. With great enthusiasm he began to proclaim the message of Christ, in such a way that it created great unrest. Just what he said we don't know, but we are told that false witnesses rose up and accused him of having spoken about the future of Christ in connection with the destruction of the Temple. As well, Stephen's defense before the Sanhedrin afterwards shows that he was not afraid to attack the Jews in their proud conviction that they had a right to eternal life simply by virtue of being offspring of Abraham. In his speech Stephen also demonstrated that the Temple must not be the object of superstitious veneration: he pointed out that God had already spoken to Israel long before the Temple was erected. We get the impression from the entire passage (Acts 7:2–53) that Stephen, more than the others, had drawn the consequences from Israel's apostasy as evidenced in their rejection of the Messiah. He saw more clearly that the New Testament church was called to a different life—that the dispensation of shadows had passed and a new covenant was offered in Christ.

Stephen's unsparing sermon to the Sanhedrin evoked a storm of hostility and hatred among the Jews in Jerusalem, especially against the Hellenists, thus especially against that part of the church that hailed from the Hellenistic world. A vehement wave of persecution ensued, one that left the apostles unmolested this time, but which cost the lives of many believers and forced many others to leave the city. But now, those who were scattered began to preach the gospel wherever they went (Acts 8:4). Thus, owing to a dispensation of Providence the grumbling of those widows ultimately led to a powerful expansion throughout Palestine and far beyond.

Still, impeding forces would appear once again later. We meet them again at that point in time when Peter began to preach the gospel to a few interested people in Caesarea. He not only spoke in the house of Cornelius but also baptized Cornelius, his relatives and friends (Acts 10:24, 48). Cornelius belonged to the many "righteous and devout" people of the time, also called "God-fearers" These were people who had come to know the truth of the Old Testament but had not yet been incorporated into the Jewish community through circumcision. It was quite something for Peter to enter the house of an uncircumcised man, to eat with him, and to baptize him. If God had not prepared him for this in a very special way[7] Peter would not have had the courage to do all this. Obeying God's command, however, Peter elicited strong opposition in the Jerusalem church that grew into controversy and recriminations (Acts 11:2, 3). With great tact the apostle managed to allay the criticism and preserve the unity of the church.

All the same, it soon became apparent that the differences were not yet settled. When Paul and company at the end of their first missionary journey

---

[7] [Reference to Peter's vision on the housetop of a descending sheet containing both clean and unclean animals and a voice that said, "Get up and eat!" (Acts 10:9–16).]

rehearsed to the church at Antioch "*all that God had done with them*" (Acts 14:27), some "*false brothers*" (Gal. 2:4) arrived from Judea (Jerusalem) with the message that the uncircumcised cannot be saved. Dissension and debate was the result, so the church of Antioch decided to consult the apostles in Jerusalem. The Jerusalem Council made a wise and cautious ruling of limited import; it was applicable only to the Gentile believers in Antioch and Syria and Cilicia (Acts 15:23), so not directly in the region where Paul was active. This decision for a while calmed the spirits, but the situation never became entirely satisfactory. In Antioch itself, some rather unpleasant things took place shortly thereafter, involving Peter and even Barnabas (Gal. 2:11–13). In the outlying churches, too, the issue continued to fester. Wherever Paul came, he met strong resistance from the side of Judaizing teachers who, entirely on their own authority, visited church after church with the goal of undermining the authority of "the apostle to the Gentiles." To the end of his life, these dangers continued to threaten Paul, and time and again he had to defend himself against the slander which these zealots for the law spread about him (Acts 21:20–21).

All this makes abundantly clear that the growth of the Early Church, too, was continually impeded. Strong forces of influence were busy night and day to debilitate activity and extinguish enthusiasm. That the work nevertheless continued to go forward was no merit of these first Christians but solely due to God's lavish care for this groping and struggling Church.

The circumcision question: church and nation

We saw earlier that one of the most difficult questions in the Early Church was that of circumcision. A proper understanding of that period necessitates probing this problem a little deeper. It concerns two fundamental issues: one about the relation between church and nation, the other about the relation between law and gospel.

The general rule in those days was that Gentiles who as proselytes joined the Jewish religion cut themselves loose, as it were, from their own national community and were incorporated into the nation of Israel. Needless to say, this practice was assailed from different quarters. Gentiles denounced proselytes for all too easily giving up their nationality, for breaking ties with their fellow nationals, and for allowing themselves to be taken up into an alien nation. The Roman historian Tacitus writes that the proselyte betrays his country and his kinsmen, and he berates such conduct as a crime against one's own people. The leadership of the Jewish people believed that a person could be saved only as a Jew, as one incorporated into the Israelite nation. In the case of mixed marriage (i.e., of a Jewish woman with a Gentile man) the couple would be required to pledge that any children at least be circumcised and so incorporated into the people of Israel. The Jewish historian Josephus relates in one place about Antioch that the Jews there constantly lured large numbers of Greeks to their worship services, adding: "making them as it were members of themselves," meaning that they absorbed them into their ethnic community.

In and of itself, this way of thinking was not unscriptural. Ancient Israel had indeed received the promises of God, and salvation is from the Jews. In those days, church and nation were not yet separated; the church functioned in the cloak of a nation, of national solidarity. Now then, such an intimate bond between church and nation contained far more elements than we often realize. All pagan religions functioned as national religions: religion was the heart of national life. This entailed that all social relations and all legal rules were determined by religion. The whole of national life was rooted in religion, so that practically every domain of life was influenced by the religious world-and-life view. That was the situation in the pagan nations surrounding Israel. Since it had pleased God to segregate Abraham and his offspring from the surrounding nations and in a very special sense to make them his own possession, religion in Israel likewise had a national character.

Purely externally, therefore, the situation in Israel governing the relation between religion and national life was identical to that in the surrounding nations. In reality, however, the God of Israel was the "God of the whole earth." Thus, in the history of revelation, Israel's isolation was only a phase. One need only open the pages of the books of Exodus and Deuteronomy to realize that indeed, also in Israel, religion affected the whole of personal and societal life. Socio-economic relations, agriculture, the legal system, in short, all domains of Israel's life as a nation were regulated from religion at the center. A person who through circumstances had been incorporated into Israel was therefore at the same time taken up in that total community in which Israel had lived for so many centuries. To be sure, partly as result of the Roman occupation of Palestine the system was no longer as closed as it once was; all kinds of influences had had a dissolving effect on it. Nonetheless, every Israelite still had a strong sense of the natural bond between religion and national life.

The Christian church at first did not realize with perfect clarity what her stance toward these things ought to be. The believers in Judea for the most part still followed the old cultic practices: they went to the synagogue and were still subject to the old Jewish legal system; in short, they still resided within the totalitarian whole of the religious national community. However, they soon faced the problem of how to view missions. Was it a grand attempt to draw the Gentiles into the Jewish nation, to uproot them from their native bonds, to plant them into Jewish soil? And did the old rule still hold that they could only be saved as members of the people of Israel? In that case the Church would be present in the world in a national or ethnic cloak and church and nation would in essence be identical. Our religion would then have continued to be a totalitarian arrangement of every relationship in life. The pagan who embraced faith in Christ ceased to be Roman, a Greek, or an Asian: he became a Jew, and from that day forward he was subject to Jewish law and absorbed into the intricate fabric of Jewish customs and regulations.

It is altogether understandable that initially people indeed tended to think that way. Believing Jews looked upon the surrounding nations (Greek: *ethnē*) as idolatrous peoples, hence the word for nation often meant pagan or Gentile. Christians, however, no longer belonged to the Gentiles, to those ethnically defined units; they had been transferred to a new nation, to the people of God. Thus, Paul writes to the Corinthians: "*Ye know that ye were Gentiles*" (1 Cor. 12:2 KJV); that is to say: you are no longer Gentiles, you are now outside that demonic power of the pagan world. Thus, when such a Christian from the Gentiles was not only baptized but also circumcised, his national place was perfectly clear: he was subject to Jewish law and absorbed into the Jewish nation. However, things were different if a Gentile was baptized only, and therefore not acknowledged as an Israelite by the Jewish authorities. Then he entered a tangled web of problems: he was still a member of his people by birth, still a Greek or a Lycaonian or Cilician, and since that national community too was religiously colored and totalitarian, he got involved in all kinds of conflicts. Naturally, he could no longer be acknowledged as a constructive member of the national community and therefore had to be thrown out as impure. He became "a man without a country." His social and political position was in limbo; he was outside the law and of no relevance. That was the great difficulty faced by the Early Church, a difficulty still encountered on the mission field today.

To be sure, we should add at once that Roman law was extremely flexible. The various peoples that belonged to the Roman Empire in many respects were allowed to keep their own legal institutions and as much as possible to practice their own religion. This policy was all the more feasible because the whole world breathed a cosmopolitan spirit, a spirit of world citizenship and toleration. The systems of philosophy in those days, the schools of Stoicism and Cynicism, were very influential and encouraged the erasure of ethnic boundaries. Religions were no longer the national possessions to the extent they once were. There was plenty of opportunity for the exchange of ideas, under the enduring protection of Roman rule. In this way the ethnic and religious systems dissolved into the international and syncretistic ethos so typical of the Roman Empire. The so-called mystery religions—we shall come back to them in a later chapter—only reinforced these developments. Eastern religions were imported into Italy and Greece and enjoyed great popularity especially in the higher circles. As a result, the position of Christians was not as vulnerable as it would have become if the different nations had still been experienced as religious units in the full sense of the word. Thus it is noteworthy that neither in Acts nor in Paul's epistles do we read much about resistance to Christianity from national considerations and loyalties. National feelings were just not strong in those days. Lycaonians and Asiatics, people from Achaia and Macedonia, had limited ethnic loyalties and saw themselves far more as citizens of the mighty international community administered by the Roman imperium. Only the Jews were an exception.

The Jewish aloofness was very much fed by Messianic expectations that filled the Jewish world at that time. In their condition of political subjugation Israel stubbornly held on to the old prophecies regarding the coming Messiah and the dominant role their nation would be given by the Messiah in the end-time. The Jews indulged in all kinds of speculations about that glorious future and yearned for the hour when all these things would be fulfilled. Many Christians from the Jews, too, seem at first to have entertained those same expectations. They knew that Messiah had already come, so they saw the work of Messiah differently than their fellow Jews. Still, many were also of a mind to regard Israel as the center of the world. Any time a Gentile came to faith in Christ, he had to be registered in the rolls of Israel, so that he would be counted among the old people of God on the day when Messiah returned. In this way Israel would become the rendezvous of the nations: people from every nation would come to be incorporated into Israel, and Israel would at last shine as the kingdom of God and his Anointed. Mount Zion would be exalted above all mountains of the world. This was the dream of these believers. It was only a dream, because hidden from their eyes was Israel's apostasy which had led to the kingdom of God being taken away from them and given to "*a people producing its fruits*" (Matt. 21:43).

The circumcision question: law and gospel

The circumcision question also had another aspect, that of law and gospel. It is well known that strong pharisaical tendencies pervaded the Jewish world of those days which influenced all life and thought. The Christian church too did not escape this influence, the more so as "zealots for the law" were received in her midst. These legalistic Christians had some understanding of the great sacrifice of Christ and of the grace of God by which alone a man can be saved. Yet somehow, they remained ensnared in the old idea that strict compliance with the Mosaic law was required for anyone who wished to be counted among God's people. They looked upon the gospel above all as a "new law," as a clarification and deepening of the law. They were governed by a slavish spirit of obedience to the law of Moses which had been in force for so many centuries.

All this need not surprise us. The Lord himself during his sojourn on earth submitted to the law. He participated in the Temple ceremonies. He kept the rules given by Moses. Nowhere did He say clearly and openly that through his death on the Cross all those old shadowy laws were fulfilled in such a way that they simply had to go. We who read the gospel in quite a different light can easily find all those places that prove this new foundation, namely the "new testament in His blood," but the early Christians did not yet see how all these things are interconnected. They still had to be led into all these truths by the Spirit of Christ, and there are many reasons why they were not as receptive to be so led by the Spirit as was called for by the new dispensation. They were too attached to the old ways, to the religion of shadows and everything that came with it, and it was difficult for them to stand fast "*in the freedom wherewith Christ has set us free*" (Gal. 5:1).

Once the question of Gentile Christians came on the agenda, several of the Church's more prominent members did see the issue correctly. Peter, who had personally received a sign from God during his visit to Cornelius, stated frankly at the Jerusalem Council that it would be wrong to burden the Gentile believers "*with a yoke that neither our fathers nor we have been able to bear*" (Acts 15:10). This did not, however, put an end to the controversy, and time and again new difficulties arose.

What undoubtedly also played a role in all these conflicts was the circumstance, still present on the mission field today, that pagan converts were strongly inclined to lapse into a kind of Christian legalism. They were used to being ruled by all kinds of regulations and stipulations, and so they expected the new religion to provide clear guidelines for every kind of life situation. They were used to having religious ceremonies at seed and harvest times, at births and marriages and sickness and death—in short, from cradle to grave they had been locked in by an overwhelming force of regulations for life, and they now wanted to receive such rules from the Christian faith. Only then would they feel safe and secure and be confident in how to live their lives. This fact, which is found on every mission field, was probably the reason why so many Christian churches of the Gentiles gave a ready ear to the promptings of Jewish zealots for the law. Paul waged a relentless struggle against this inclination, a struggle already reported in Acts but especially evident in his epistles. Just read the letter to the Galatians, for example, and you can understand how difficult it was to do battle with a tendency found among both Christians from the Jews and Christians from the Gentiles.

All this is enough to impress upon us that missionary activity by the Early Church did not exactly move on a path strewn with roses. There were problems of daunting magnitude. There was hesitation, dearth of insight, internal division, distrust, suspicion. We are all the more amazed—and envious—that the work nevertheless made such rapid advances.

Missions without missionaries

In two different places Luke relates the sober but highly significant fact that those who were scattered abroad "*went everywhere preaching the word*" [literally: "evangelizing"] (Acts 8:4, and again at 11:19). Between these two passages we learn several important facts, such as the conversion of Paul, the baptism of Cornelius, and so on. Apparently, Luke wants us to be aware that while important events were taking place in and around Jerusalem, the word was spreading without letup. The process of gospel missions by non-ordained and unsponsored preachers had taken off and could not be stopped.

All scholars who have described the initial developments of the Early Church are agreed that this calm, spontaneous, largely hidden proclamation of the gospel by roaming refugees contributed by far the most to the rapid spread of the message of Christ in such a brief time period. Latourette states without reservation:

> The most important assistants for the spread of Christianity do not appear to have been persons who made it their occupation to preach or who spent at least most of their time at it, but they turn out to have been men and women who earned a living in an ordinary worldly occupation and spoke of their faith to anyone they met in a perfectly natural manner. When the pagan author Celsius expresses his contempt for a religion that is spread by wool merchants and tanners and other uneducated folk who attract children and teach ignorant women, then Origen does not deny that this indeed happened.[8]

Adolph Harnack, author of the well-known work *The Mission and Expansion of Christianity in the First Three Centuries*, notes the same fact: "The most numerous and successful missionaries of the Christian religion were not the regular teachers but Christians themselves, by dint of their loyalty and courage." And in another place Harnack assures us that there is no doubt in his mind "that the great mission of Christianity was in reality accomplished by means of informal missionaries."[9] The strongest statement has been made by Roland Allen, whose valuable study *The Spontaneous Expansion of the Church*, specifically mentions this phenomenon of "lay" missionaries and recommends it for our own times.[10]

The Book of Acts, too, shows clearly how the work of these "scattered" believers bore much fruit. At first it was particularly the "lay" preachers fleeing

---

[8] Kenneth Scott Latourette, *A History of the Expansion of Christianity*, 7 vols. (New York: Harper & Brothers, 1937–1945), I, 116.

[9] Harnack, *Mission und Ausbreitung des Christentums*, I, 377–78 [Eng. trans., I, 458, 460].

[10] Roland Allen, *The Spontaneous Expansion of the Church* (London: World Dominion Press, 1927) [American edition: Grand Rapids, MI: Eerdmans, 1962].

from Jerusalem that preached the gospel wherever they went. Their work is credited with the birth of churches in Samaria, Phoenicia, Cyprus, and Antioch. Next to these persecuted evangelizers there must also have been others from the start who spread the message of Christ. In Acts chapter 9 we read of a group of disciples in Damascus (vs. 19) and of churches throughout all Judea and Galilee and Samaria (vs. 31). When Peter made the rounds among the scattered believers, he was able to visit saints who lived at Lydda as well as at Joppa (vss. 32, 36). On his first missionary journey Paul must have already come upon disciples on the island of Cyprus, even though no mention is made of them in Acts. The tentmaker Aquila and his wife Priscilla were active preachers; in the interim between Paul's second and third missionary journey this couple did some very basic work in Ephesus for example. Towards the end of his third missionary journey Paul encountered groups of believers in Tyre and Ptolemais (Acts 21: 3, 7). And there may already have been Christians living in Sidon too (Acts 27:3).

Similar information is found throughout the New Testament. On his third journey, when Paul was staying in Corinth, he wrote a letter to the church in Rome, without our being told how the church got there. When Paul personally traveled to Rome he came across brothers in Puteoli (Acts 28:14). Everywhere in the New Testament we notice that surrounding the work of the apostles was missionary activity by itinerant preachers branching out in all directions. It was a growing, flowing stream, a stream that continued to spread long after the death of the apostles.

A spontaneous spread such as we find in the Early Church comes about, of course, along natural lines. A stream follows a natural channel. It is important to take note of that because it may just contain the key to the secret of the rapid spread of the gospel in the first centuries. Looking at the scanty data in the New Testament, we readily arrive at the following results:

a) A natural channel for the stream of faith was offered by the synagogue. Wherever synagogues were located and where also were found a group of proselytes or God-fearing Gentiles, there a natural opportunity offered itself to proclaim the gospel. As we shall see later, Paul made ample use of this opportunity.

b) Another important channel was the family setting. More than once we read that someone came to the faith "with his entire household" (for example, the jailer in Acts 16:30–34). The household included not just the family in the narrow sense but as a rule also the slaves: they too belonged to the household and shared in the privileges enjoyed by the head of the house.

c) Now and then we learn that collegiality, too, was used as a means to preach the gospel. It turns out that the centurion Cornelius had a "devout soldier" as his aide-de-camp (Acts 10:7), whom he charged with the important task of sending for Peter. From other reports, too, we learn that in the army one soldier would tell another about the way of salvation. In Corinth, Paul in the most natural manner made the acquaintance of his fellow tentmaker Aquila, and this collegial bond was the means by which Paul gained an opportunity to bring the good news. There must have been many more such contacts, and they were used by God to spread the word of Christ over an ever wider geographic area.

d) Next to that, no doubt, was the neighbourhood. The believers in a city would soon be inviting their neighbours to tell them about this new thing that had come into their lives. One can well imagine that this gave rise to the so-called "house churches" that are so frequently mentioned in the epistles of Paul. Thus, in Rome the indefatigable Aquila, together with his no less hardworking wife Priscilla, appears to have gathered a church in their house that met on a regular basis (Rom. 16:3–5).

e) Finally, many random encounters of every description will have served for passing on the message. "Chance" encounters like that would have included travel companions. Paul spoke to the crew and the passengers of the ship as he sailed for Rome. Commercial ties and other possibilities would have been utilized for the purpose as well. Once you desire to preach the Word, daily life offers you so many channels that every day new lines of communication open up.

Naturally, a spontaneous "evangelistic campaign" like this was not entirely without its difficulties and dangers. It was not always certain that the "pure gospel" was being preached. Even with the best of intentions, untrained preachers could get caught in all kinds of misunderstandings. They started conversing with pagans who were far better grounded, and then it could happen that they were not always aware of the consequences of their own words. It is not inconceivable that they might have become infected with ideas and concepts of pagan origin without realizing what dangerous territory they had entered.

A second, no less serious difficulty was that the dissemination of the gospel became somewhat disorderly. There was no supervision. Circles of believers arose that were completely out of touch with the churches founded by the apostles. The Christian community lacked cohesion and at times faced insoluble problems. Unquestionably, this was another danger that must have been keenly felt in those early decades.

As we prepare to study the significance of Paul as a missionary figure, we must not for one moment isolate his labour from all that unorganized and unsupervised evangelistic work by lay preachers. Paul is surrounded by it; we can understand his labour only if we see him working amid all those running rivulets of spontaneous gospel preaching as they arose in households and marketplaces, in barracks and aboard ships.

We know but little about the content of the proclamation by these refugees. In general, we may imagine it was in the spirit of the words that Philip, one of the "seven men," addressed to the Samaritans. A brief summary of what Philip preached is recorded as follows: "*. . . he preached good news about the kingdom of God and the name of Jesus Christ*" (Acts 8:12). This accords with Acts 11:20 where we read that those who were scattered because of the persecution in Jerusalem spoke to the Hellenists, preaching the Lord Jesus.

From these meager data we can at least be sure about a number of points. First, the message of the refugees was of a highly personal nature: it was focused on the *person* of Jesus Christ. They preached Jesus Christ—the Lord Jesus. No doubt they did this while making use of all the stories about the work of Christ that were already in circulation before the Gospels were written. "Jesus is Lord! He who believes in Him is saved, in life and in death. He is the Redeemer sent by God." We may assume that this initial proclamation of the gospel was devoid of dogmatic formulations. It was too early for that, too immediate, and too unreasoned. Nor was it a type of preaching that focused on "experiences," on subjective feelings, but rather on objective facts.

Secondly, the "*Name* of Jesus" was put in the foreground. It is the name so often shown in Acts as having great hidden powers. The apostles, as early as their first appearance before the Sanhedrin, were commanded "*not to speak or teach at all in the name of Jesus*" (Acts 4:18). The name of Jesus was for the first believers a daily wonder. In that name the lame were healed (3:6); to suffer shame for that name was a joy (5:41); before that name the powerful of the earth were powerless. Whoever believes in the name of Jesus, not as a magic formula but as the name of Him who came into the world for our salvation, that person is richer than all noblemen: he has access to the eternal fountains of God's power and God's blessings.

In the third place, it is striking that the content of that first proclamation was "the kingdom of God." A kingdom presupposes a King; it demands obedience, submission, humility. Simon the Magician had supernatural powers at his disposal and acted like a king. He called himself "*somebody great.*" Everybody in Samaria, from small to great, paid attention to him as the "power of God" because "*for a long time he had amazed them with his magic*" (Acts 8:9–11). Philip, by contrast, spoke of a kingdom of God, a kingdom in which we remain servants, in which we do not command but comply.

Lastly, it is evident that these refugees brought all these things as an evangel, as good news. Their sunny words brought joyful tidings. They themselves had found peace and so they could be messengers of peace. Their whole life radiated a holy joy, making them effective agents for bringing the gospel to others.

That is the picture we get of the quiet, hidden work of these "ancient heroes." They probably didn't rack their brains over the question of circumcision and all the consequences attached to it. According to Acts 11:10, they initially talked only to the Jews, but after that they also, without hesitation and without needing a vision, proceeded to share the message with the Greeks, that is to say, with pagans! In that respect they lived out of the naiveté of the faith; they could not keep silent about it and that is why they saw no boundaries. They themselves were not aware of the world-historical significance of what they were doing. Neither did they seem to worry at all about whether these first converts from the pagans had to be circumcised. They simply accepted them as fellow believers and very likely baptized them as well. When later Barnabas came to Antioch we do not read that he proceeded to baptize them; presumably they had already been baptized. In other words, they simply bypassed that great problem of circumcision that would later exercise the minds of so many. They did so completely unconsciously, without fathoming why they did so. It needed an apostle like Paul to take what they did spontaneously and provide the rationale and warrant for it from the depth of Scripture. The issue was decided by the facts before theological discussion about it had commenced. "*The hand of the Lord was with them,*" writes Luke (Acts 11:21), as if to say: despite their lowly, uneducated status, they were guided by the Holy Spirit onto a path that would much later be acknowledged generally as the right path.

To summarize what we have found thus far, it appears that the apostles and elders in Jerusalem were at first very hesitant about missions among the pagans. Not until the apostle Peter was compelled by God did he visit a God-fearer and baptize him. That was still a God-fearer, hence someone who in his heart already sympathized with the Jewish faith. The Jerusalem circle was not yet ready for the work of missions among "pure" pagans because they still had not fully understood what Jesus had so clearly taught them. The main problem holding back "foreign" missions was the question of circumcision with its double aspects of the relation of church and nation and the relation of law and gospel. Finally, we discovered that when the "official" circles still hesitated and took no action, common lay preachers, roaming refugees, in holy naiveté took the steps that no one in Jerusalem dared make. They passed on the gospel by word of mouth without worrying about the problem of circumcision, simply driven by love for their Saviour. The upshot of it all, as we can now see, was that God incorporated the quiet labour of those refugees into the great work that He purposed, namely the proclamation of the gospel among all peoples. That work He achieved by calling and equipping Saul of Tarsus, his "chosen instrument" (Acts 9:15).

2. Paul and the Itinerant Preachers

The background of Paul's activity

If we want to get an idea about Paul's missionary activity, we do well to approach him as a man who was called by God to be an apostle in a most unique way and who was parachuted into the great forward movement of the Church of those days. In other words, Paul's lifework arose from the process of the spontaneous spread of the gospel by refugees and would soon take up its central position there.

To see Paul's work in this way, we need to recall in outline the beginning of his ministry. We are not going to try and sketch the apostle's personality nor form an idea of his character. We need mention only a few traits, since they are essential for understanding the career that followed.

Paul was born in the Cilician city of Tarsus, where he also spent his early years. Situated along a major military road that led from western Asia Minor to Syria, Tarsus was visited daily by merchants, soldiers, and imperial messengers, as well as all kinds of teachers—traders in intellectual and spiritual goods. These things must have aroused in young Saul something of an awareness of world citizenship. People in Tarsus were keenly aware of being included in the dynamics of the times; they heard the heartbeat of Rome's world empire. In his parental home Saul would have been initiated into the faith of his fathers according to the strict tradition of pharisaism. He learned the law of God and the countless rules of tradition; here he fought his first struggles to behave as a "child of the law." In the life of the apostle later, we can still see an afterglow of the tension he had lived through in his youth.

Saul of Tarsus is a man who thinks in terms of countries and continents, a person who is enchanted by the call of distant lands, someone who feels the powerful pull of the vague and the unknown. He always wants to go farther, travel to new regions, visit new cities, follow new roads. But sometimes, in the midst of his wanderings, he will come to a sudden stop, overwhelmed by nostalgia for Jerusalem, the city of his ancestors. Halfway a missionary journey he will suddenly be overcome by a deep longing to go up to the Temple and mingle with the festive crowds. Paul understood, better than all the other apostles, that the time of shadows was past, that the temple worship with all its rituals had been fulfilled in Christ and therefore had lost its meaning. Yet the love of his heart still went out to it as to a beautiful memory from days long gone by. In his later years, Jerusalem again and again became for him a source of disappointments; he was never trusted there—always watched with a measure of suspicion, even by brothers and sisters in the faith. Yet the pull of Jerusalem remained a force in his life that he was never able to shake.

Paul's conversion took place in the days when believers fled Jerusalem to escape persecution and began to disperse into various directions, preaching the word from place to place. Mostly simple, poor people, artisans or merchants, they found time in their activities to proclaim the name of Jesus Christ. They were displaced persons who found no rest anywhere and who traveled along all roads to glorify their Master.

Already in the days of his conversion Paul received the assurance from Christ that he would be called "*to carry my name before the Gentiles and kings and the children of Israel*" (Acts 9:15). These words contained his calling as an apostle, even though no one at the time realized it. Several years would have to pass before his apostolic office was widely acknowledged. For the time being, in people's eyes Paul remained an ordinary believer, someone who was captivated by Christ and naturally felt impelled to serve Him. In that respect he was no different than those roving refugees who preached wherever they went even though they held no ordained office and no one had sent them.

Still in Damascus, our fresh convert, a former pupil of Gamaliel, spoke up in the synagogue, and he did it with the fire and the knowledge of Scripture so characteristic of him in all his later work. In one of his letters Paul relates that he had gone to Arabia in those days and from there had returned to Damascus. When he once again addressed the Jews in the synagogue, they plotted to kill him and he was let down in a basket through a window in the city wall and so escaped (Acts 9:23; Gal. 1:17; 2 Cor. 11:32, 33). Difficult days lay ahead of him. In Jerusalem he was at first not admitted into the circle of the brothers until Barnabas succeeded in getting him admitted to the council of the apostles. He was allowed to stay in Peter's house for a couple of weeks, but here as well the situation got too dangerous and at the express command of Christ he got out of the city and went to the land and the task that God would show him (Acts 22:18–21). And so he left, as so many before him had been forced to leave the city where their Master had been crucified. Now Paul himself had become one of those roaming refugees, one of the many dispersed believers who had been scattered because of the persecution that arose over Stephen (Acts 11:19).

It will probably always remain a puzzle how it came about that Paul did not do then what the other fugitives did, namely roam through the country and preach the word. Did he not feel strong enough yet? Was he disappointed by what he had experienced in Damascus and Jerusalem? Did he realize that the fact that even fellow believers only half trusted him constituted too serious an impediment and that therefore a number of years first had to go by before any work by him could be blessed and bear fruit? Or, now that new light had come into his life, did he feel obligated before all else to go and tell his own father and mother and relatives and friends about the change that Christ had brought into his life? Whatever the case may have been, we watch him depart for Caesarea and from there cross over to Tarsus in Asia Minor. The brothers who accompanied him from Jerusalem to Caesarea evidently assisted him in word and deed in this painful moment in his life. They were the ones who "*sent him off to Tarsus*" (Acts 9:30) after advising him to first go back to the city of his birth.

We have reason to believe that Paul spent quite a number of years (probably about nine) in Tarsus.[11] Those years are shrouded in mist; not one fact about them is told us. He must have worked very hard throughout that period, and we can be sure that he never passed up an opportunity to talk about his Lord and Saviour. But more important than what he did outwardly in that time is what he personally relived and reconsidered inwardly. There in Tarsus he must have wrestled with the Judaism of his day. He understood the danger that pharisaism posed for the young Church. He fully grasped the problem of circumcision, the crux for missions at the time. When we later see Paul on the mission field, acting with a firm hand as someone who knows what course he must follow, then he owed this resolution undoubtedly to what he had thought and struggled through in those quiet years of isolation. "The genesis of Paul as a Christian and as a theologian must be sought in that period that is obscured to our eyes."[12] In his letters the apostle recalls once or twice what he went through in those years. In one place he writes in some detail about how "fourteen years ago" (that must

---

[11] For a chronology of the life of Paul, see my handbook *Geschiedenis der Godsopenbaring: Het Nieuwe Testament* (Kampen: Kok, 1938), II, 533 and 654.

[12] Joh. Weiss, *Das Urchristentum*, 151.

have been during his stay in Tarsus) he was entrusted with "unspeakable" revelations, but also how he was then tormented by Satan yet triumphed through Christ (2 Cor. 12:1–10). No doubt there were more things that he "received from the Lord" in those days (1 Cor. 11:23).

If we wonder why God did not call Paul to his apostolic work earlier, we should remember that the Church of his day was not yet mature enough to receive him. Before there could be a place in the Church for a man like Paul, not just Paul had to mature but so did the Church. Missions among the Gentiles could not freely spread its wings so long as the Church was fixated on the idea that the gospel was intended for the circumcised and that it had to be addressed to those who wished to be incorporated into Israel. God does not seem to have wanted Paul to be the first to bring the gospel to the Gentiles; there were others who were privileged to do so. Fugitives from Jerusalem were the first preachers to the pagans. God could not use Paul for that work because Paul enjoyed too little trust from the brothers in Jerusalem. Not until the word had begun to spread was the time right for a mature Church to have room for a matured apostle.

The names of those who preached to the Gentiles in Antioch are not mentioned. Luke does show us how that work was prepared very slowly and gradually. On the day of Pentecost the message of Christ had been directed at Jews and proselytes, Philip had preached among the Samaritans, and Peter had spoken to the God-fearers. It was all a long introduction to missions among the pagans. Now, in Antioch, lowly brothers were the first to dare speak of Christ to the Gentiles. Thus, they merely took the next step on the course God had caused his Church to follow. Harnack has pointed out that we have good reason to locate the names of these first preachers among the Gentiles mentioned in Acts 13:1, where we hear of the "prophets and teachers" active in Antioch. Of the five there mentioned, we know that Paul and Barnabas came to Antioch only later. It is not impossible that the other three names, namely Simeon who was called Niger, Lucius of Cyrene, and Manaen, were among the charter members of the church of Antioch. This is all the more probable because Luke informs the reader in Acts 11:20 that it was men from Cyprus and Cyrene who had been the first to speak to the Hellenists about the faith. Since Lucius evidently hailed from Cyrene, it is easy to see that he must be counted among those "men from Cyrene." That said, it is clear that we will not get beyond conjectures.[13]

Once missions among the Gentiles had become a fact, the church in Jerusalem faced exceedingly difficult issues. How were these Gentile brothers and sisters to be viewed? Should they be welcomed with gladness as fellow believers? Or at all events should they be required to let themselves be incorporated into Israel through circumcision? Up till then the Church had carefully preserved this bond with the synagogue. However, if uncircumcised pagans were taken up into the Church, in the long run a radical break with the synagogue would be unavoidable. Could they risk that? Furthermore, how was the lifestyle of these Christians from the Gentiles to be regulated? Were they to hold to the rules about fasting, about the sabbath, about cleansing rituals, in short to all those numerous regulations that bound the life of every devout Jew? What was the relation of these Christians from the Gentiles to the temple worship and its ceremonies? Was there not the danger that two kinds of Christian churches would develop, one that perpetuated the bond with the old, with temple and synagogue, and one that would be entirely separate from it? Contemplating the consequences of what had been done in Antioch in perfect naiveté, the leaders of the Jerusalem church felt confronted by an endless series of exceedingly weighty and all but unsolvable problems.

Apparently, the whole issue was discussed at length in the church at Jerusalem. Earlier, when Philip had preached in Samaria, the council of the apostles had sent some delegates to witness the work; this time the whole congregation was involved. This indicates that the Jerusalem church had grown more mature and felt responsible as a body for what was happening beyond the city. The deliberations resulted in commissioning Barnabas, who was himself a Cypriot and possibly acquainted with the Cypriot brothers who had laboured in Antioch, to go and find out what was going on. This Barnabas, as Luke assures us, "*was a good man, full of the Holy Spirit and of faith*" (Acts 11:24). In Antioch he conducted himself with great care and tact, and when he saw that he had to do with people who were sincerely dedicated to serving the Lord, he realized at once that he was not allowed to return to his commissioners but instead had to stay where God had brought him. In many respects these young and inexperienced

[13] Harnack, *Mission und Ausbreitung des Christenthums*, I, 51 [Eng. trans., I, 59].

Christians from the Gentiles needed guidance and reinforcement, so it would have been irresponsible to leave them on their own. And because Barnabas soon noticed that his strength was inadequate for this ever-expanding work, he decided to invite Paul of Tarsus to come over and assist him.

It was in this way that God recruited Paul for the forward movement of His Church. Paul now came into contact with the work of the "scattered" believers, the uneducated brothers who had proclaimed the gospel from pure love of Christ. These brothers had absolutely no idea of the difficulties they had unleashed and of the prospects their labour foreshadowed. It was at this point in time that God injected Paul into the movement. The time was ripe. Paul's lifework was attached to the work of those scattered believers and taken up into it. Everything that Paul now undertook was as it were an extension of what those brothers had begun. Soon it would become apparent that he was assigned a unique role in that movement. More and more of the work of outreach began to be concentrated around his person. He became the focus, as it were, of all this work.

In the opening verses of Acts 13 Luke describes how the work of missions was carried forward out of Antioch. We shall probably never learn how the Holy Spirit's command came to the church of Antioch. From the few data recorded we get the impression that this command was first given in the circle of the five prophets and teachers. We read that the Holy Spirit spoke to them "*while they were worshiping the Lord and fasting*" (Acts 13:2). These words alone present us with difficulties. We do not know what is meant by "worshiping the Lord."[14] But "fasting" also raises questions. In the Early Church fasting is always mentioned in connection with important acts, such as the appointment of elders (Acts 14:23). Did the fasting by the leaders in Antioch also have such a concrete goal? Johannes Weiss does indeed suggest this as a possibility. He believes that these prophets and teachers of Antioch consulted together about the question whether the work of missions should not be extended further. Was Antioch to be considered the end point of the forward movement or should new regions be visited? That was the question that occupied these men and together they asked

---

[14] The Greek verb used here is *leitourgein*, from which our word "liturgy" is derived. Some commentators read this word as a technical term, i.e., as referring to a *worship service*, including the sacrament of the Lord's Supper. See Kirsopp Lake, *The Beginnings of Christianity,* 5 vols. (London: Macmillan, 1933), vol. IV, note on Acts 13:2.

for light from God after "*worshiping the Lord and fasting.*" The Spirit's command must have come to them as an answer to their "fasting and worshiping." Weiss also bases his conjecture on the fact that the Spirit says that Barnabas and Paul were to be set apart "*for the work to which I have called them.*" These words do not at all specify the kind of work intended, nor that it would be done outside Antioch. The vagueness of these words, Weiss suggests, would seem to indicate that they are to be viewed in connection with a question that was living in the hearts of those who received the command.[15]

It seems to me that there is something to be said for this reading. In any case, the circle of the prophets and teachers must have entertained the idea that Antioch should not be the end point of the progress of the gospel, but only a transit station. The Spirit's words responded to what was in their hearts. The Spirit did not give this command in Jerusalem, because Jerusalem was not ripe for it. In Antioch, where love of missions shone brightly, the Spirit's command would have been understood and obeyed.

Yet there is something in the Spirit's directive that surprises us. It was not Paul and Barnabas who had been scattered and then "*went about preaching the word*" (Acts 8:4). It was not Paul and Barnabas who had brought the gospel to Antioch. They came only later, entering as it were upon the labour of others. Now then, the remarkable thing is that not those first preachers and not those men of Cyprus and Cyrene were set apart for the work, but the latecomers were chosen for it. The work would be carried forward, but there was a change of personnel. From now on, other men would travel the world and preach the word. Nor were these other men spontaneous preachers. Rather, they would be empowered and commissioned. They would be sent out, not scattered or dispersed. Thus, these verses teach us that things were taking a turn, that the initial course would be continued, but in a different manner than it had commenced. It is quite possible that the original founders of the church of Antioch were disappointed that they could not volunteer their time and effort for the work. They too had to learn the lesson that God calls people according to His wisdom and pleasure, and that He chooses those whom He wants to use for the work according to His purpose.

[15] Joh. Weiss, *Das Urchristentum*, p. 151.

To what extent the congregation of Antioch played a role in all this remains unclear. After the word of the Spirit has been received, we read again of prayer and fasting—no doubt by the same circle of prophets and teachers who had done so the first time. Yet there is reason to assume that the whole congregation participated this second time. It is highly unlikely that a serious matter such as sending out two teachers would have taken place without the congregation's involvement. This is the more likely since we keep reading in Acts that in those days all kinds of weighty matters were discussed in meetings of "*the whole assembly*." It is safest to assume, therefore, that the entire circle of believers in Antioch were involved in sending them off, including the laying on of hands (Acts 13:3).

And so Paul and Barnabas departed from Antioch. Luke does not emphasize that the congregation had a part in all this. All he says by way of summary is: *So, being sent out by the Holy Spirit . . .* (Acts 13:4). Thus, not the Church but the Spirit is depicted for us as the great Sender. The two men who were sent had no instructions from any church; they went out as people who had no other calling than to proclaim the gospel. And so they were totally given over to the Holy Spirit, to be used for the work to which He had called them. As Luke records with a pithy expression: "*they had been commended to the grace of God for the work*" (Acts 14:26).

The style of the work

The missionary work of Barnabas and Paul was the continuation of the work of those "scattered" fugitives about whom Luke reports that they "*went about preaching the word*" (Acts 8:4). At the same time, it is noticeable that the missionary activity of Paul began to exhibit more and more a distinct type, one with its own style, distinguishing it from all others. To see this, let us carefully collate the data recorded by Luke about Paul's journeys. When we do so we are able to discern four characteristic features: (i) increasing concentration, (ii) a principled basis of operation, (iii) maintaining continuity, and (iv) repeated recruitment of fresh human resources.

(i) increasing concentration

When we compare the three missionary journeys we are struck by the phenomenon of increasing concentration. More and more these journeys are losing the character of "going about preaching the word" and are marked by the concentration of all activity on a few places.

In a certain respect, the first missionary journey is a case apart. Paul was accompanied by Barnabas, a man older than himself and one who already had a long career behind him as a minister of the gospel. Even though it is not expressly mentioned, it stands to reason that Barnabas had a strong influence on the whole itinerary. His influence is at once apparent when we see the two preachers taking off for Cyprus. Barnabas himself hailed from Cyprus; that is where his relatives and friends lived, so naturally his heart felt a special pull to that island. What may also have influenced this choice of destination is the fact, as we recalled above, that several "scattered" brothers from Jerusalem had already gone and preached there (Acts 11:19). Paul and Barnabas could reasonably expect, therefore, to meet up with a small group of believers on the island. It would have appeared essential, first of all and most of all, to strengthen these young believers in the faith.

Barnabas and Paul left the island again at the very moment when the work on Cyprus reached its highpoint, namely, when Paul struck Elymas the magician with temporary blindness and the proconsul Sergius Paulus "*believed when he saw what had occurred*" (Acts 13:12). Should that word "believed" be taken in the profound sense of a permanent change of life? Or was it more an intellectual decision on the proconsul's part that the word of Paul was more trustworthy than that of the magician? In either case, it is remarkable that the two missionaries failed to avail themselves any further of the great opportunities offered them. In later years Paul systematically avoided Cyprus. He revisited every other church, but he never sailed for Cyprus again. It seems to me that this was more than a coincidence. Paul sought out the great trade routes and the centers of commerce and government; he looked for the places where the gospel could spread out in all directions. An isolated island like Cyprus, a small world all by itself, cramped his style. His heart went out to the continent, where endless opportunities were beckoning.

Once arrived in Asia Minor, the two workers traveled from city to city, following the passable roads that led through the mountainous landscape. They preached the word in every place they came. They did not stay anywhere for very long, nor could they linger in places for any length of time, for everywhere they were threatened by the hatred and jealousy of the Jews. Continuing further east, they turned in the direction of Tarsus, as though they were planning to return via Tarsus to Antioch, whence they first set out. Had that plan been carried out, the first missionary journey would have taken on the circular form that can be seen in the later journeys. For some reason, however, our itinerant preachers turned back at Derbe and retraced their steps along the same route they had come: they went down to the coastal town of Attalia. Undoubtedly, this return journey over Lystra, Iconium, and other places is related to the fact that the young circles of believers in those places had a hard time of it. They incurred the full weight of the hatred of the Jews that was intended for Paul. The threatened position of these churches made it imperative to visit them again and to encourage them. To shore up their defenses, Paul and Barnabas "*appointed elders for them in every church*" (Acts 14:23).

If we now sum up the first missionary journey as a whole, it cannot escape us that there was no single city in particular on which the two preachers concentrated their efforts. They traveled the roads, they preached the word everywhere, but we do not as yet find any trace of focusing their labour on a few central points.

This changes already on the second missionary journey. In passing, we note that Barnabas no longer accompanied the apostle, as a natural result of which this second journey gained a stronger Pauline character. For reasons told in Galatians 2:13 and Acts 15:36–39, Paul distanced himself from his earlier coworker. For when Peter came to Antioch and avoided eating with uncircumcised believers, Barnabas "*was led astray*" by him, something for which Paul sternly rebuked him. A short time later, a difference of opinion with respect to John Mark resulted in the two men judging it the better part of wisdom no longer to journey together.

Paul's second missionary journey is marked by a very special openness to the guidance of the Holy Spirit. At one time Paul was prevented by the Spirit from preaching the gospel somewhere, at another time the Spirit did not permit him to pursue a specific itinerary. Finally, in Troas, he received a definite indication of the goal that God had in mind for him.[16] We can tell that the apostle, knowing that God was using him for a work of world-historical significance, made sure he was fully alert to the guidance of the Holy Spirit. Other things, too, showed the same submission to the divine will. In Athens, when it soon became clear that the climate for fruitful labour was most unfavorable, Paul at once left the city and made for Corinth. In Corinth he received a divine command that he must not allow himself to be discouraged but should stay there and keep up the work, because, said the Lord, "*I have many in this city who are my people*" (Acts 18:9, 10). In this way Luke, as he describes this journey, lets us know every now and then that from day to day the apostle surrendered himself into the Lord's hands.

Paul stayed and worked in Corinth for a year and six months (Acts 18:11). That fact alone is of great significance. A totally new element now entered missionary journeys: quietly labouring for many years in one and the same place. The early fugitives roamed the land and preached the word. Paul now looks for important centers and stays there for months and years on end, working steadily.

Moving on to the third missionary journey, we are immediately struck by the fact that the new element of concentration is becoming even more pronounced. The apostle travels directly to Ephesus and stays there without interruption for no less than three whole years. A church is established there that develops into a focal point for missionary activity throughout the province of Asia. It is no exaggeration to observe that the third missionary journey was given over to Paul's labour in Ephesus; anything else the apostle did on this journey was not so much reaching out to establish more churches as consolidating churches that had already been established.

Summing up, we can conclude that through the guidance of the Holy Spirit missionary activity developed gradually from roaming through the country to a conscious, concerted effort to concentrate on a few exceedingly important and strategic points. That is the first characteristic feature that we can detect in the work of Paul.

---

[16] [Reference to Paul's nighttime vision of a Macedonian man urging him, "Come over and help us" (Acts 16:9).]

(ii) based on principle

A second feature that calls for our attention is no less valuable. It was clear from the very beginning that the apostle had to map out a course of action with respect to the question of working among circumcised and uncircumcised people. The scattered preachers had initially brought the word to Jews and proselytes, but quite naively they had ended up preaching also to the Gentiles. With that, a most important step forward had been made, but obviously this deed also had to have a basis in some foundational principle. What was the future attitude to be towards Gentiles who showed an interest in the gospel? If they asked to be baptized, could that be done on condition that they be circumcised and so incorporated into the nation of Israel? Or was that not required? And if not, then on what grounds were these considerations to be based? Numerous thorny questions presented themselves that were of paramount importance for the practice of preaching the message. Until they had clarity about the principles to follow, practical action had to wait.

This situation highlights a significant component of Paul's work. Through the power of the Holy Spirit, Paul guided the young Church from ambiguity and vagueness to clarity and conviction about the basic principles of missionary activity among the Gentiles. In his hands the problems associated with it gained unsuspected depth and beauty. He articulated the theological considerations and formulated the practical guidelines that retained their validity for the ages. This is not the place to discuss these things at length, but we shall have to come back to them in a later chapter where we examine the Pauline letters. In the present context we shall limit ourselves to a few comments about missional practice.

On the first journey, Paul and Barnabas confined themselves to preaching in synagogues. We do not read of any deliberate attempts to seek out the Gentiles, but of course when the proconsul himself desired to hear the word the two missionaries did not pass up the opportunity.

This changed already in Antioch of Pisidia. Here too Paul and Barnabas began their work in the synagogues, but as soon as it became apparent that the Jews were not receptive to their message, "*they shook off the dust from their feet against them*" (Acts 13:51) and resolutely turned to the Gentiles. The apostle himself formulated the principle behind this move in the following words: "*It was necessary that the word of God be spoken first to you, but since you thrust it aside and judge yourselves unworthy of eternal life, behold, we are turning to the*

Gentiles" (Acts 13:46). The apostle would remain faithful to this principle for the rest of his journeys.

This principle was gradually developed further. Everywhere Paul first turned to the Jews, and only when they rejected him did he turn to the Gentiles. Usually it turned out that the Jews were little inclined to listen to him, whereas the God-fearers, and especially the women among them, gave the apostle a ready ear. On the second missionary journey, the synagogue at Thessalonica proved very hostile, while the synagogue in Berea showed a great deal of interest and "*received the word with all eagerness*" (Acts 17:1–12). It was in Athens that Paul for the first time took his stance in the midst of the pagan world. There was a synagogue in that city, but apparently it was not suitable for outreach, so that he felt called to turn directly to people who had never heard about the Word of God. From that point on, missions among the Gentiles unfolded more and more into an independent component of Paul's work. Thus, in Corinth, when the Jews rejected him, he "*shook out his garments*" (Acts 18:6) and began a strictly separate mission among the Gentiles. The same scene is repeated later in Ephesus: when the Jews opposed his message, the apostle, in search of a different venue, rented a hall from a certain Tyrannus and began to preach to the Gentiles quite apart from the synagogue (Acts 19:9).

In other words, Paul's missionary journeys show that initially he worked solely among the Jews, that later the synagogue was used as a gateway from which to sally forth into the pagan world, and that at a still later stage work among the Gentiles developed into a completely separate activity. This whole development did not take place from pragmatic considerations but was consciously taken, step by step, on the basis of principle. The apostle understood that first of all the Jews in every place had to make up their minds about their Messiah who had been crucified in Jerusalem. If they committed the same sin as their leaders, they would suffer the same rejection that their leaders had incurred. Later, Paul expressed all these things with the image of a tree and its branches: natural branches are broken off if they bear no fruit, and new branches are grafted onto the tree. In this way the rejection of Israel means "*the reconciliation of the world*" (Rom. 11:15).

(iii) maintaining continuity

The apostle Paul practiced continuity in all his work. He did not roam from place to place but carefully tended the ties once made. On his very first journey we see him turn back from Derbe to revisit the churches he had recently founded. He repeatedly visited every group of believers he had assembled, and when unable to pay them a personal visit he tried to keep up contact by sending them a letter. The unorganized missions of the first phase were replaced in Paul by a purposeful bringing of the gospel and a continuous building on the foundations once laid. As we can gather, the apostle had an astonishing memory for people and their names; years later he would still remember persons he had once met. That is evident from the many names he mentions in his letters and from the cordial way he speaks about them. This strong bond with brothers and sisters in the faith must have stood him in good stead for the considerable task of maintaining vital connections with all the churches. But given the pressing circumstances that he worked under, those connections would sometimes be a reason for real "*anxiety*" (2 Cor. 11:28). Nonetheless, it must have been a constant source of solace for the apostle to know that all those churches held him in their thoughts and prayers with love and gratitude.

And so we see Paul's activity before our eyes, not as a restless journey back and forth, but as a deliberate continuation of contacts once made.

(iv) repeated recruitment of fresh human resources

Finally, Paul's work is characterized by the fact that time and again he recruited new helpers. He had not yet started this on his first missionary journey when he was in the company of Barnabas, but as soon as he was all by himself and could develop his own style, he gathered a number of young men around him and involved them in his great assignment. Thus, already during the second journey he engaged various aides. These numbers increased considerably on the third journey, with the result that at the finish of that journey the apostle was surrounded by a whole group of dedicated companions.

As we look over this group, we notice that it was composed of people from many different places. The first coworker on the second journey was Silas; he hailed from Jerusalem (Acts 15:22) and joined Paul at the start of that journey. Silas probably did not come along on the third journey. Later, we find him in close contact with Peter (1 Pet. 5:12).[17]

[17] [The Silvanus mentioned by Peter is generally assumed to be Silas; he is also mentioned in 2 Cor. 1:19.]

Paul's second companion is Timothy. He met this young man in Lystra and persuaded him to follow him. Before joining the apostle on his journeys, Timothy first professed his readiness to serve Christ in the young church of Lystra. Furthermore, hands were laid on him by the council of elders and by Paul himself, to dedicate him to the work to which he was called (1 Tim. 4:14; 2 Tim. 1:6).

Paul's third companion on his second missionary journey was probably Luke, the author of the Book of Acts. He seems to have joined the apostle from Troas onward. In Corinth, the apostle made the acquaintance of Aquila and Priscilla. This believing couple put themselves at his disposal with great loyalty. They performed valuable work in a variety of places where they went to live. In his letter to the Romans, Paul writes that they "*risked their necks for my life*" (Rom. 16:4).

During the third missionary journey, many other aides affiliated themselves with Paul. Although the name of Titus is not mentioned in Acts, there is reason to believe that Titus accompanied Paul from the very start of this journey. Paul used him for important tasks related to conditions in the church of Corinth (see 2 Cor. 7).

Acts 20:4 lists the names of a large number of men who had joined the apostle. Among them was Aristarchus, a believer from Thessalonica, who apparently had been a travel companion of Paul for a long time already and who was among those dragged to the theater in Ephesus (Acts 19:29). We also hear of Gaius, who hailed from Derbe, and of Tychicus and Trophimus from the province of Asia (Ephesus).

Quite a number of other names are found in the epistles. We hear of Urbanus, "*our fellow worker in Christ*" (Rom. 16:9), of Demas, who had been an aide at first but later "*loved this present world*" (Philem. 24; 2 Tim. 4:10). As well, the names of Apollos, Artemas (Titus 3:12, 13), Crescens (2 Tim. 4:10) and many others are mentioned in the epistles as Paul's co-workers.

We learn from all this that the apostle did initially take on the work alone or with one or two companions, but also that he gradually drew many others into the work. He became the focal point, as it were, of a widespread movement; in a short time his preaching radiated out in all directions. This phenomenon is so important that we are to view it as more than purely coincidental; this was, rather, an essential element of Paul's method of operation.

Paul and his aides

In order to grasp the importance of this phenomenon, we should begin by explaining more closely the place of all those fellow workers in the apostle's plan of action.

The first thing that strikes us is the warm tone in which Paul would write about his helpers. He had all kinds of names for them, names he used for indicating the nature of his relationship with them. In 2 Corinthians 8:19 he writes about a brother (whose name he does not mention) as his "*travel companion*." In many other places he uses an image borrowed from the workshop and talks about his "*fellow workers*" (Rom. 16:3, 9, 21; 2 Cor. 8:23; Phil. 2:25; Philem. 1, 24). The apostle very often depicts their common labour as a war, and he refers to his aides as "*fellow soldiers*" or comrades-in-arms (Phil. 2:25; Philem. 2). On one occasion he borrows a metaphor from agriculture and speaks of one of his helpers as a "*yokefellow*" (Phil. 4:3). On another occasion the memory of shared jail time or persecution makes him call his aides "*fellow prisoners*" (Col. 4:10; Rom. 16:7; Philem. 23). The conviction that we are all slaves of one Lord and Master, Jesus Christ, causes him several times to confer on each of his aides the title of *syndoulos*, i.e., fellow slave, fellow servant or bondservant (Col. 1:7, 4:7).

Now then, all these people were constantly at the apostle's beck and call. In one sense they were his personal servants; he sent them wherever he wished. On the second journey he left Timothy and Silas behind in Berea (Acts 17:14). On the third journey he decided to send off to Corinth, first Timothy (1 Cor. 4:17, 15:10), then Titus (2 Cor. 12:18), to pacify the church there. Later, he left Titus behind on Crete (Titus 1:5), then summoned him again to Nicopolis (Titus 3:12). From Rome he sent for Timothy, who was then staying in Ephesus (2 Tim. 4:9). In this way the apostle disposed of all these human resources as instruments in his hand, and he could rest assured (with one or two exceptions) that each one of them was eager and willing to be of service. From the few data available it is evident that these aides were useful for the apostle in a twofold respect: first, they had been preachers themselves who had proclaimed the gospel to outsiders, both Jews and Gentiles, and thus had been employed in outreach; at the same time, they were often called upon to give leadership to the newly established churches, or to bring order to places threatened by dissension and confusion.

To be sure, this does not mean that these fellow workers were fit only for giving assistance and never exhibited any personal initiatives. About some of them, at least, we get the impression that they went their own way quite independently and only on a few occasions worked closely with Paul. Aquila and Priscilla, for instance, followed their own course, even as they continued to stay in touch with Paul. Titus apparently went on a missionary journey to Dalmatia of his own accord, and Crescens likewise went to Galatia on his own initiative (2 Tim. 4:10). In other words, these people were not just will-less tools in the hands of Paul; at various times they acted quite independently, although they did maintain their ties to the apostle and were available to him for work that he judged more urgent.

Looked at in the light of missionary activity in those days, this situation clearly constitutes an important feature in the Pauline approach. When Paul first got involved, the Church had already gone on the attack. It was spreading in all directions, thanks to the believers dispersed from Jerusalem. The offensive had been launched on all fronts, even though the advancing columns had little contact with each other. Paul recognized both the great value and the danger of this spontaneous expansion. On no condition would he want to disrupt this simple, fruitful work. He realized all too well the incalculable benefit of having this evangelism continue quietly and calmly from one locality to another. Missions in those days was not like missions in the modern sense of the word: work that is carried on by educated and trained fulltime workers, salaried by a sending church. Back then, resources such as we have, like schools and hospitals, were not available. Most churches were very poor and in not a few instances did not fully understand their task to preach the gospel. Thus, the future of the Church depended on that quiet, spontaneous spread by those anonymous fugitive preachers who plied some trade or other and simultaneously brought the gospel from town to town. A man like Paul, for all the work he would do and for all the journeys he would make, still could not allow that earlier phase to be eclipsed, nor would he allow all the work to start concentrating on him alone.

So he stimulated it. That is what is so grand about Paul's missionary work. He was too strongly convinced of the need of that spontaneous activity to want to cross it for even one minute. He himself arose as it were from the circle of itinerant preachers who traveled from town to town. Granted, what no one realized at first was that he had received a very special apostolic calling from Christ himself. But charged with that calling he stepped into the midst of the current, and everywhere around him he unleashed a mighty stream of spontaneous activity. He entered the advance party of the Church and transformed it into a purposeful forward march of a large host, with himself at the head. He saw the best lines of attack. He knew the weak spots of the enemy. He laid out the operational strategy. He brought leadership and depth to the great work. And in order that the Church would know what her task was in the great battle of the spirits, he saw to it that the work would increasingly be borne by the Church herself. To each of these points we shall devote some more space.

As noted, Paul stimulated the spontaneous proclamation of the gospel to an unusual degree. This is immediately apparent from the fact that in every church he visited he stirred people into action. In Lystra he drafted Timothy, from Derbe he took Gaius along, and in Ephesus he engaged Tychicus and Trophimus. In short, in every place where he laboured he recruited people for the work. From the moment he touched them with his magic wand they all became comrades-in-arms in the great spiritual war. Not that they laid down their old vocation. About Aquila and Priscilla we may assume that they continued to work as tentmakers also after their conversion, and many of these aides to Paul will have earned their living in a similar fashion. But in their earthly calling they now became *perigrinantes propter Christum*: "pilgrims for the sake of Christ," as the Dominican fathers used to call themselves many centuries later.[18]

In the second place, Paul increasingly *centralized* the work. The early phase of preaching the gospel lacked order and regularity; it had no system or policy. That all changed once Paul took things in hand. The people that would henceforth be engaged received some sort of training. They first traveled with the apostle for a long time before he deposited them on an independent, lonely post. Paul did not hesitate to charge even young men with heavy responsibilities. There is no doubt that when Timothy was called from Lystra, he was still very young; yet many years later the apostle still writes to him: "*Let no one despise you for your youth*" (1 Tim. 4:12). Nonetheless, on that very first missionary journey that Timothy was called to join, he was left behind in Berea to work on his own. Paul did make sure that Timothy was not left all by himself on that lonely post, but it does show his great confidence in the young man in that he was willing to charge him with such responsible work.

---

[18] Cf. Latourette, *A History of the Expansion of the Church*, II, 324–325.

The apostle to the Gentiles trained his other helpers in a similar fashion. He recruited them, placed them somewhere at an important post, and then later had them rejoin him under his paternal care. In this way they were gradually formed into sound and capable fellow soldiers. When they were working somewhere all by themselves, Paul did not abandon them for a moment. Even from jail he continued to provide them with help and advice. The entire missionary campaign thus took on something like the shape of a star, with the apostle in the center: from there he would personally dispatch his counsel and commands in all directions.

Obviously, this *deepened* the work immensely. The earlier days of naïve, spontaneous, improvised preaching were over. Missions now acquired some level-headedness, something like a very conscious sense of responsibility for the task. The Gentiles now heard the message not as the spin-off of practical circumstances, but as the result of a sober-minded approach, in obedience of faith. When it was decided that a Gentile who came to faith in Christ needed to be baptized but not circumcised, the decision was based on principle. The letters that were sent to Timothy and Titus are very informative about the type of directives that Paul was accustomed to give to his helpers; they deal with all kinds of questions about ecclesiastical organization, but also about doctrine and liturgy, as well as ethics and the Christian lifestyle.

Finally, Paul linked the work of these helpers with the Church in her *institutional* form. We broach this subject with considerable hesitation because we still know so very little about the officially ordained functions in the Early Church. At this time, the charismatic offices—i.e., the functions that rested on "singular" gifts and special talents endowed by the Holy Spirit, such as prophecy—were barely distinguished from the ordinary offices.[19] That is why we can still have only a poor understanding of church life in that time period. There are, however, a few indications that can help us form some idea of it.

The first thing we should note is that the apostle's most prominent helper was Timothy, with whom he had a very special bond and who had been called to his work through the laying on of hands by the elders of the church of Lystra (1 Tim. 4:14; Acts 16:1–3). Though still young and inexperienced, he was entrusted in that solemn moment with an important office, one of broad import

---

[19] Cf. A. M. Brouwer, *De kerkorganisatie der eerste eeuw en wij* [The organization of the Church in the first century, and us] (Baarn: Bosch & Keuning, 1937), ch. 10.

and great responsibility. Knowing about Timothy that he was "ordained," as it were, in a solemn gathering of the church for the task of assisting the apostle, we have every reason to assume that the other helpers—Titus, Gaius, Aristarchus, and many others—were similarly set apart by their home church for "official," ordained service. In other words, it is very likely that those aides of Paul were not just "unofficial" lay preachers but were set apart in a church meeting for the work of missions. Not that they were "chosen" or "elected" by the congregation. At least, about Timothy we know that his ordination followed upon a "gift of prophecy." Paul as a rule probably chose his helpers personally, yet he also set great store by the fact that these helpers were put at his disposal by a church and that they were ordained for their office in a congregational meeting.

The exact nature of their office is, again, in many respects unknown. From Paul's second letter to Timothy we get the impression that his office was denoted as "evangelist": Paul encourages him to fulfill his ministry by doing the work of an *euangelistēs* (2 Tim. 4:5). Ephesians 4:11 mentions the office of evangelist immediately after that of apostle, hence it appears to have been held in high esteem by the Early Church. The fact that Philip ("one of the seven" mentioned in Acts 6:5), is likewise called an *euangelistēs* in Acts 21:8 indicates that the title was applied not only to direct aides of Paul and the other apostles but also to men who operated more or less on their own. At least, we are not aware that Philip had a special relationship with any of the apostles. However all this may be, it is no doubt highly significant that the aides of Paul were given a special title and that they were installed in their office by the Church. Thus, their work was the work of the Church; the Church acted through their mediation. We do not read that Timothy ever rendered an account of his work in the particular church where he was ordained; on his journeys he did not feel himself to be in the first place a missionary from Lystra; his work was too universal for that. Nevertheless, the fact that at one time he had been set apart by a particular congregation remained an important fact throughout his life. That Paul reminded him of that fact many years later signifies that the apostle himself deemed the event of his ordination to be of fundamental value for all the work performed by his beloved son Timothy.

The second crucial aspect we should take note of is that Paul's helpers were in constant touch with the life of the churches. The early refugees may have roamed the land and preached the word, but their intent was never to establish churches. Paul himself realized that it was essential for even the smallest circle of believers to be given some form of organization. Already on his very first journey he appointed elders in Lystra, Iconium, and Antioch of Pisidia, in what were then still very small circles of believers (Acts 14:23). He instructed all his pupils and aides to work along the same pattern. When circles of believers arose all over the island of Crete (we don't know how that came about), Titus received the explicit mandate "to appoint elders in every town" (Titus 1:5). No sooner were elders in place, than the evangelist stepped back, and a church entered a regular course of life. Even later, however, evangelists continued to give guidance and leadership. In the church of Ephesus, which undoubtedly had many members by that time, Timothy occupied a position of authority. He was not to lay hands on anybody rashly, without due diligence (a clear reference to the installation of elders); he was given instruction about the kind of people who were eligible for the office of elder and deacon. In short, his position in the church of Ephesus continued to be of far-reaching influence. This exceptional authority entrusted to the helpers of the apostles was related to the plenipotentiary power which they had received from them. They acted with an apostolic mandate and therefore with apostolic authority. Given the fact that the apostles did not arise from, nor were chosen by, the Church, but inversely, that the Church was built on the foundation laid by the apostles, these aides of the apostles in the nature of the case cannot be put on a par with any office-bearers of the present time.

Summary

Paul's work arose from the work of the "dispersed" roaming preachers. Paul himself was sent out from a church that had grown out of that spontaneous labour of the fugitives. Thus, his entire work must be seen against the background of this natural expansion of the Church.

Paul keenly sensed the immense importance of this natural expansion. He understood that the apostles could fulfill their calling to preach the gospel to all creatures only if they recruited a host of men as well as women (think of Priscilla). The entire Church was to continue its forward movement without interruption.

However, Paul was just as keenly aware that this spontaneous, carefree work ran the great danger of confusion and disorder. He did not restrain the flood of the spiritual movement of his day but stepped right into it and personally unleashed a force that was noticed throughout the then known world.

3. The World of Paul's Struggles

The demise of the national religions

Throughout the ancient world and no less throughout the mission field today, the phenomenon of religion is most intimately tied to the concepts of nation and national community. It is in religion that a nation, tribe, or ethnic group professes its deepest unity: religion is the bond that unites all.

It goes without saying that the close tie between religion and national community can occur in all kinds of forms. Among so-called "primitive" nations there often is no clear consciousness of being a national community; the various tribes live their separate lives, frequently covering only a few small villages. Nonetheless, a tribe will consider itself the heart of the world. The tribe's religion then comes down to this, that its people relate directly to the divine forces in nature of which they believe they are the offspring. In this way religion creates a tight bond around the tribe; members feel united with one another because they share the same divine gifts and powers. This view is also related to the near inability to recognize members of another tribe as belonging to the human race: they stand outside the religious bond in which one lives from day to day, and they have no part in the forces over which one disposes; in short, they constitute a kind of intermediate species between man and animal. This is how countless tribal communities in all parts of Asia and Africa used to think and still think.

Nations that have moved on to a grander, more comprehensive concept of people or nation generally arrive at similar conclusions. To be sure, with them the religious element does not remain so strictly limited to a small group of people; their vision is broader. But now it is *the nation as a whole* that is deemed bearer of the religious goods; the nation as a whole is deemed to have a special tie to the world of the gods; the nation as a whole therefore also knows itself to be strictly bound to the religious customs, mores, and precepts of the generations that have gone before. Such a nation, too, has the ineradicable tendency to view itself as a kind of divine kingdom on earth, and consequently it cannot regard and respect other nations and peoples as its equals. Those other nations are at bottom but barbarians, people of weird customs and strange languages, people who have no part in the religious community in which one lives and breathes. To the present day we encounter these and similar ideas everywhere on the mission field, and in the nature of the case they are the very ones that cause missions many difficulties and a lot of trouble.

When we, informed by this knowledge, look at the world in which Paul worked, it strikes us that his situation differed considerably from what we are accustomed to run into. A quick glance into the Book of Acts can convince us of this difference and open our eyes to the very special nature of the religious questions facing Paul. Consider the few occasions when he came face to face with the pagan world of his day as Luke has described them for us. Keep in mind that Paul usually met the pagan world via the synagogue and was seldom confronted by that world in its brute forms. In the synagogue he addressed not only Jews and proselytes but also "God-fearers," people who were of pagan background, but who had already received so much instruction in the truth that they had learned to bow before the God of Israel. Whenever the apostle had to do with those people, his message of course focused on evidence from the Scriptures that Jesus is the Christ. Quite different was the reaction as soon as he bypassed the synagogue and approached pagan circles directly.

Four such encounters are mentioned. On his first missionary journey Paul appears to have preached the gospel in the market square of Lystra. In those day the market or *agora* was the place in the city where people met, did business, and exchanged ideas; where spiritual and political leaders addressed the crowds to win their support. Thus, the marketplace was a very fitting place for the purpose of preaching the gospel, particularly in those cities that had no synagogue or where the synagogue did not offer sufficient opportunity to interact with the Gentiles. Paul's preaching in the market square of Lystra and the miracle he performed there made a deep impression on the populace (Acts 14:7–18). They immediately took Barnabas and Paul to be *theophanies*, manifestations of the gods, and without hesitation they got ready to pay the two visitors divine homage. The gods they identified them with were Greek deities; thus it was the Greek religion that the apostle encountered here. However, in the land of Lycaonia the Greek religion had taken on a distinct local color: it included legends about appearances of Zeus and Hermes in human form, and the crowds apparently viewed the actions of Paul and Barnabas in the light of those old tales. Their reaction creates the impression that they were totally sincere and convinced about their view of things. Here Paul stood face to face with paganism in all its vibrancy and tenacity. In Derbe, too, Paul in all probability preached in the market square—at least we read that he preached the gospel "*to that city.*" Here we do not read of any pagan reactions to his message.[20]

On the second missionary journey the apostle had a fulsome encounter with paganism. That was in Philippi, a Roman colony in Macedonia, where he had first approached some proselytes and God-fearers who regularly came together at a "place of prayer" by the riverside, there being no synagogue. But then the whole city rose up against Paul after he had healed a slave girl possessed by a spirit of fortune-telling. He was accused of disturbing the peace and advocating "customs that are not lawful for us as Romans to accept or practice" (Acts 16:20f). This whole reaction to the work of Paul has something unsavory and untruthful about it. Pretending to be defending ancestral customs, his opponents were acting from purely egoistic motives, driven by anti-Semitism and love of Mammon. Philippi was hardly the place for a genuine confrontation between the gospel and traditional paganism.

The third missionary journey saw a similar occurrence in Ephesus. Patron of the city of Ephesus was the Greek goddess Artemis (Diana to the Romans). Her image purportedly had fallen from the sky in the form of a sacred stone, which was held for safekeeping by the city. Ephesus accordingly was known far and wide as the city especially consecrated to worship in the Temple of Artemis. Thus, here Paul again came face to face with Greek religion, but here too the Greek religion had taken on local color. The Artemis that was worshiped in Ephesus was not the ancient Greek goddess of the chase but the mother of life, the goddess of fertility, the source of all well-being and prosperity. When Paul began his work in Ephesus, he first looked for a point of contact in the synagogue. Not until the synagogue proved unwilling to receive the word did he turn directly to the pagan circles of the city. He regularly gave "lecture courses for seekers" in a rented hall (Acts 19:9). Thanks to this systematic approach his sphere of influence grew by the day, contributing not a little to the growing intensity of opposition. All this ended in the infamous riot instigated by Demetrius the silversmith. Luke describes the riot not without humor; he clearly brings out that Demetrius and his fellow artisans tried desperately to make it seem as though they were worried about the honor of the great goddess, but in

[20] [Luke simply writes that they "*made many disciples*" (Acts 14:21).]

the meantime their greater worry was the loss of business in the sale of souvenir shrines. Hence, the riot was not a spontaneous reaction but an organized demonstration. A large part of the crowd that amassed in the theatre soon did not know why they had gathered there. For some two hours on end they cried "Great is Artemis of the Ephesians," but the volume of their clamor was not commensurate with the depth of their conviction. Most conspicuous, in other words, is again the unsavory and untruthful character of paganism's resistance.

The encounter Paul had in Athens takes place in an entirely different context. Although there was a synagogue in Athens (Acts 17:17) which provided an opportunity to penetrate the pagan world by way of the synagogue, Paul nevertheless chose to go directly to the marketplace to preach the gospel. That was contrary to the fixed rule and Luke takes care to state the reason for it. Paul departed from the tried method because "*his spirit was provoked within him as he saw that the city was full of idols*" (Acts 17:16). The reaction that followed upon the encounter on the *Areopagus* (Greek for "Mars Hill") deviated in several respects from what we found elsewhere. Here in Athens the entire conversation remained within the academic sphere. Paul was forced to deal with philosophers from different schools who had invited him to the Areopagus. So in Athens we don't hear of spontaneous reactions from the crowd; we hear only of discussions among learned men.

Reviewing the four encounters, we can say that there was genuine contact with popular religion only in the case of Lystra in the interior of Asia Minor. There, religion was still the national religion, spontaneous and alive, supported by all members of the populace. In Ephesus and Philippi we get the impression that paganism had become more artificial; it was still supported by tradition, but it no longer exhibited vitality and vigor. And in Athens a reaction from the national religion was entirely absent. All this is an indication that in those days the ancient national religions had begun to lose their moorings, that they were no longer rooted in the national community, and that countless disintegrating factors were beginning to assert themselves. Paul came up against what Karl Barth has called a "chronically sick" religion, a religion that had lost all confidence in itself.[21] This phenomenon is the reason why only with the greatest

---

[21] Karl Barth, *Die Lehre vom Worte Gottes. Prolegomena zur kirchlichen Dogmatik* (Munich: Chr. Kaiser, 1932–1938), I/2 (1938), 345 [Eng. trans., *Church Dogmatics* I/2 (Edinburgh: T. & T. Clark, 1944), 316].

caution should we draw parallels between what Paul encountered on the mission field and what we experience every day. When it comes to religion, the world in which Paul laboured had a very special character. That is why we will not understand the apostle's working method unless we gain a clear idea of that special character.

The new world

The Greek world in which Paul worked as he visited its far-flung urban centers already had a long and remarkable history behind it.

In ancient times, the country of Greece was made up of more or less independent city-states, i.e., small political units concentrated around a walled town as the bearer of authority. Nature itself encouraged this fragmentation. High mountains and deep valleys, separated by narrow passes, made it difficult to penetrate from one region to another. In each of those valleys a distinct life unfolded where independent thought and ideas could develop. In a quite natural way, local gods were venerated everywhere, deities that were worshiped only in a specific place and venerated as the patron god or goddess of that particular city-state. Cultic communities rose up around old temple structures, and each of those communities represented a distinct and separate type.

In the history of Greece this provincialism more than once proved disastrous. Each city-state often cared little about the fate of the other city-states and was more concerned with the pure preservation of its own interests. As a result, relations between the city-states were often marked by envy and enmity. Sometimes, under the threat of a common enemy, the spirit of splintering particularism would be abandoned for a while and the approaching enemy would face a united front. But time and again, after the Greek world had raised itself to the level of national unity, it sank back into its old error, and the seeds of jealousy and ambition resumed their fatal influence.

Despite all this, we can talk of a "Greek spirit" from ancient times onward, a spirit that permeated the different states as a life-giving force. Exactly how it affected them all is hard to trace, but that it existed from of old cannot be disputed. The great poet Homer, who through his famous epics exerted an incalculable influence on the whole of Greek culture, undoubtedly contributed not a little to opening the eyes of the Greeks to what united them. Homer's fascinating stories ignored all local deities: "His gods are pan-Hellenic, Olympian."[22] Thus at an early stage already, despite all that provincialism, the road lay open to the broad and encompassing universalism so characteristic of Greek thought and creativity.

Upon close inspection we cannot help but notice that the Greek spirit concealed a host of contradictions. In ancient Hellas a delicate sensitivity to harmonic beauty, to careful equilibrium, was closely connected with an unrestrained desire for ecstatic intoxication, for the flush of *enthousiasmos* (literally: being filled with or possessed by a god). Excessive veneration of athletic feats, a veritable cult of the male physique, flourished next to a deeply rooted conviction that the body was no more than the prison of the higher, deeper forces of the soul. A sense of scintillating humor lay enmeshed in a profound feeling of the tragic in human life. Ancient, esoteric rituals were carefully observed, but next to that we see the unfolding of an irresistible tendency to freethought, to philosophical reflection on the mysteries of the universe. Nowhere else in the world have fanciful myths—dressed up in the garb of subtle stories that explain the rise and demise of the world—grown so early into logical theories as in that same Greece where, regardless of all that philosophical reflection, the old polytheistic paganism survived from generation to generation. Near-paralyzing dread of demons, fear of the irrational and inscrutable will of the gods, and haunting anxiety about the all-threatening power of fate lived alongside resonant and radiant songs about the joy of life and the beauty of the world.

On more than one occasion still another contradiction influenced the course of events in a compelling way. Very early on, a democratic constitution developed in several of the old city-states, one that gave considerable authority to the *dēmos*, the people. Early on, the city of Athens, which often took the lead in the concert of the city-states of Greece, also led the way in increasing the power of its citizens. Its popular assembly gained supreme authority. The Assembly of all freemen could hire and fire at its pleasure the officials that ran the state. "Our government," said Pericles, one the greatest personalities in the history of Athens, "is called a democracy because it is a form of government not of the few but

---

[22] Erwin Rohde, *Psyche: Seelencult und Unsterblichkeitsglaube der Griechen* (Leipzig: Kröner, 1903), 27 [Eng. trans., *Psyche: The Cult of Souls and Belief in Immortality among the Greeks* (New York: Harper & Row, 1966), 25].

of the many." Indeed, the *dēmos* had the highest authority; it decided on war and peace, on all important political and economic affairs.

This organization of government undeniably entailed risks. Unrestrained popular influence often led to unbridled anarchy, accompanied by confusion and power vacuums. The Assembly easily allowed itself to be dominated by considerations of sentiment; it was often the welcome prey of golden-tongued adventurers. Whoever expects good governance from rule by a popular assembly will run into grave disappointments, as Athens did in several precarious moments in its history. Small wonder that thoughtful citizens of Athens made the search for the best form of government an abiding concern. Sometimes, in reaction to the disintegrating forces of populism, they threw themselves into the arms of the most unvarnished tyranny, to a Tyrant responsible to no one, a personality to whom they would entrust the affairs that the Assembly had not been able to handle. Athens never achieved the proper equilibrium between full-fledged democracy and absolute tyranny; it remained in search of it throughout the centuries. Its greatest thinkers, Plato and Aristotle, threw themselves with all the power of their intellect on the problem of the state, but they too failed to find the correct formula. They never rose above the narrow construction of the city-state as the ideal of political community.

World history shows an exceedingly complicated correlation of political events and cultural development, a correlation that has so many facets that it cannot be captured in a single formula. Political triumphs (or setbacks) and military victories (or defeats) can sometimes be highly stimulating for the unfolding of a people's cultural life, but at other times they can also cause untold damage. It is not always the case that a people which gains the upper hand in a military sense will also set the tone culturally. Sometimes the very opposite happens: a comparative study of the political and cultural aspects of world history makes clear that their influence on each other defies definition. The history of Greece is adequate proof of this.

In the fourth century before Christ, Greece was united under the scepter of the Macedonian king Philip. Despite initial resistance the Greek city-states were soon at peace with this new arrangement. They realized that a monarchical form of government had advantages not available either to democracy pushed too far, or to rule by a tyrant. When sometime later, Alexander of Macedon began his triumphant campaigns in the East, the Greek world largely supported him. The vast conquests of the young monarch brought new worlds within their horizon, opening vistas never dreamed of. Peoples they had earlier spurned as barbaric now became known as cultural powers with which it was worthwhile exchanging intellectual and spiritual goods. From that time dates the phenomenon of Hellenism: that peculiar mentality that grew up after Hellenic thought and achievements had come into contact with the religious cultures of the East.

Hellenism kindled many new forces. In Persia, Syria, Palestine, Egypt and other countries, Greek customs were adopted, Greek ideas became familiar, the Greek language developed into a world language that was spoken in every large urban center. Inversely, Eastern notions and customs traveled westward, Oriental writings were translated into Greek and found their way to the academies of the Greek cities. The earlier particularism began to be viewed as outdated and was more and more curtailed; universalist tendencies gained ground: people felt the need to be taken up in broader communities. When Alexander died young, great political confusion ensued, yet the monarchical idea was never abandoned again.

Meanwhile in the West, the Roman Empire began its period of great expansion. It had been held back for many years by wars with Carthage in North Africa, but once that city was laid waste Rome was free to turn eastward. Macedonia was defeated and amalgamated. Using its organizational skill, Rome made use of the rivalries between the city-states to firmly establish its authority over them, ending Greece's existence as a political entity. The old city-states were given a certain measure of freedom and self-government within the framework of subservience to the Empire.

During the period of Roman rule, the entire Greek world developed an increasing sense of world citizenship. People felt taken up in the vast community of the Roman Empire and began to view themselves as well as other peoples from a different perspective. The universal forces which had of old been latent in the Greek mind now blossomed forth. Borders that had for centuries separated people from people now appeared very porous, unable to stem the flow of intellectual goods and spiritual values. Narrow particularism made way for cosmopolitanism, for the idea of a world state, the *oikoumenē*, the inhabited world of which each ethnic nation was but a province. This political constellation offered unprecedented opportunities for the spread of Greek culture. While Latin kept its status as the official language, the Greek language soon became the language of everyday, one that was used even by Roman officials in the provinces of the Empire. Greek customs penetrated to the far corners of the Empire, and in Rome itself men of learning and the arts turned to Greek thinkers and sculptors as their models. Former national cultural goods were more and more forgotten. A new age beckoned, one that no longer had room for whatever had kept people apart. Despite the powerful and often arbitrary nature of rule by Roman governors, it was widely felt that the Empire offered opportunities that were far superior to what had formerly been available. Inevitably, these sentiments also found expression in the intellectual and spiritual movements of the age.

Intellectual-spiritual movements

The age now entered was rich in intellectual-spiritual movements. Various schools began to flourish. For our purposes it is important to examine the most prominent ones. Besides cosmopolitanism, there was liberalism, moralism, syncretism, and mysticism.

Cosmopolitanism

The growing sense of being world citizens was very much stimulated by the political events mentioned above. Intellectually it was underpinned and endorsed by Stoicism, one of the most powerful philosophical currents of Hellenism. This was all the easier since in Stoicism western and eastern thought found each other. Countless predecessors of this school hailed from the East, from Asia Minor, and from other oriental provinces. They imbibed Greek thought and identified themselves with it. They blended and melded what the nations had been seeking and groping for.

Early Stoicism, dating from between roughly 300 and 150 B.C., already contained many ideas that fostered this cosmopolitanism. It taught that this whole world in which we live is animated by a divine force, a *pneuma* or spirit that fills all creatures. This divine force is at the same time the ordering principle, the *Logos* (universal reason) that sustains the harmony of all opposing forces and so makes this world an efficiently furnished world, a world in which everything is in its right place. Particularly in man these divine forces achieve lofty heights. To be sure, man is also host to all kinds of passions and desires that perturb his inner life and prevent the divine spirit from entering. However, through detaching himself from joy and suffering through *apatheia* (non-feeling), man is able to overcome these retarding forces in himself and to find that perfect inner peace that is born wherever the divine Logos has become the all-sustaining force.

This pantheistic scheme of thought, found in all kinds of variations among Stoic thinkers, leads automatically to cosmopolitanism. It loosens man from his ethnic bonds: no longer is the tribe considered divine, but humanity as a whole is regarded as filled with divine forces. The different nations, each with its culture and worldview, are but specifications of the one human life. The divine spirit has embodied itself, as it were, in mankind as a whole. That is why humans should become more conscious of their unity as the human race and strive to get to know and view each other as brothers who belong together. The founder of Stoicism, Zeno (336–264 B.C.), like so many Greek thinkers, tried to formulate a *politeia*, a theory of the state in which his ideas and ideals are crystallized into a political system. The little of it that has survived shows how far it differs from the politics of Plato and Aristotle, both of whom assumed the city-state, the *polis*, as the normal form of government. Zeno by contrast takes his starting point in humankind, in which all those city-states are taken up as closely connected cells. Here, all citizens, freemen and slaves, men and women, are united by the one indwelling divine Logos. Temples devoted to local gods no longer belong in the ideal state. They are replaced by the idea that the world itself is the temple where the divine spirit dwells and works.[23]

This cosmopolitanism of course entailed extremely important consequences. As we saw, the question of slavery now appeared in a much different light. Among all nations, the phenomenon of slavery in one way or another is justified in religious terms, in line each time with the prevailing worldview. So it was in the Greek world. Once the idea takes hold that a tribe has a special relationship with the gods, the subjects of subjugated peoples will be viewed as inferior beings, as a race that lacks an intimate relationship with the gods and is therefore destined to a life of servitude. The cosmopolitan spirit that permeated the later Greek world did not, it is true, abolish slavery, but it did exert a favorable influence on the fate of slaves. In many families, slaves were included in the

---

[23] Cf. P. Wendland, *Die hellenistisch-römische Kultur in ihren Beziehungen zu Judentum und Christentum* [Greco-Roman culture in its relations to Judaism and Christianity], 3rd ed. (Tübingen: P. Siebeck, 1912), chap. III.

household, they were given certain rights, and sometimes they enjoyed great honor.

The same is true of the position of women. Women too were raised to a position of honor when the idea of world citizenship gained ground everywhere. Zeno even wanted women to dress like men, to demonstrate that all humans were equally animated by the gods. Of course, such a far-reaching egalitarian approach proved impossible in practice, but the fact is that in the later Greek world women gained a different position and began to be regarded as equals alongside men.

If the cosmopolitanism of the early Stoics had something surreal and fairy-tale-like about it, once the Roman Empire began to spread its might over the entire known world it seemed as though the old ideals might become reality. The later Stoics tried to adjust the Stoic principle more concretely and realistically so as to be in line with actual conditions now that those conditions had brought the ideal of world citizenship so close.

All sorts of factors in Hellenistic times reinforced this cosmopolitanism. In the first place, ease of travel offered the different nations many opportunities for exchanging ideas and customs. Roman legions maintained a measure of peace and order in the provinces, which made travel safe and accessible to all. And people did travel a lot in those days! An inscription on the tomb of a Phrygian merchant of the second century informs us that during his lifetime this man had made the trip from his country to Rome seventy-two times. Such wanderlust would be entered into the record books even today.[24] Very well, one glance into the Book of Acts is sufficient to make us realize that also in Paul's days traveling was a very common activity. Just tracing the careers of Aquila and Priscilla shows that this couple on several occasions in a short period of time moved from one country to another. And we have similar reports about other associates of Paul. On his many journeys, Paul himself had no trouble finding a ship to take him to wherever he wanted to go. Travel had become an everyday affair. There are accounts from that time about a large fleet of well-rigged ships that carried a considerable part of Egypt's annual grain harvest to the city of Rome. Some of these vessels measured sixty meters in length and could take on a cargo of 1,500 tons. While in former centuries travel by sea was always a risky venture, by Paul's

---

[24] See Harnack, *Mission und Ausbreitung des Christentums*, I, 25 [Eng. trans., I, 21].

time a sea voyage had become, though still not entirely hazard-free, a journey that could be undertaken confidently, without undue worry.[25]

Obviously, such intense traffic was also of influence on the intellectual and spiritual traffic between peoples. Not just merchants and officials traveled the roads of the Empire, but also teachers—philosophers who proclaimed their theories from city to city, among them Stoic scholars and Neoplatonic thinkers that visited different countries and contributed to the growing awareness that one idea, one worldview was shared by all.

After the many wars that had plagued the centuries before Christ, the new conditions were experienced by many as a relief. Peace and order that prevailed throughout, the unity of all those many peoples that were included in the Empire, the opportunities for intellectual exchange—all these were deemed valuable goods that held great promise for the future. The church father Origen praised the unity of the Empire as one of the most important means used by God to put the whole world in touch with the gospel. The sole emperorship of Augustus, he wrote,

> fused together into a single monarchy the many peoples of the earth. It would have been an obstacle to the spread of the gospel if the entire world had been divided over many kingdoms, for it would have seen men everywhere engaging in war, fighting in defense of their native countries, which was the case before the times of Augustus.[26]

Established by past political events and affirmed by contemporary philosophic thought, Christians experienced this cosmopolitanism as a benefaction and blessing of God.

Liberalism

Characteristic of the entire Imperial Age was a mixture of humanism and individualism. By *humanism* we mean the cluster of ideas that sees in a human person special gifts and talents that are of divine origin and infinite value: man

---

[25] See Alfred Edersheim, *The Life and Times of Jesus the Messiah* (1884; New York: Longmans, Green and Co., 1917), 60. See also Ludwig Friedländer, *Sittengeschichte Roms* (Vienna: Phaidon, 1934), II, 131.

[26] Origen, *Contra Celsum*, 2.30.

is seen less as a member of the cosmos, as a tiny atom in the vast universe; he is abstracted as it were from the soil on which he grew and is made into something special and unique, an integral unity that possesses, in and of itself, all the powers and strengths that it needs. By *individualism* we mean the attitude that tends to look upon the individual apart from the community: here, man is no longer viewed as a cell in the great body of the people; he is not a member of the national community anymore but an independent unit, a persona, a personality.

Once again we see a clear break with the older worldview. The old city-states had no room for individuals: the state regulated every detail of their lives. In Plato's ideal state, too, the individual is entirely absorbed into the whole; he is obliged to view his person and his possessions as belonging to the state. Even today, among many nations in the Far East and other parts of the world, we meet the idea that a person should only be regarded as a member of the whole; all his thoughts and actions are encompassed by the national ethos, the national religion, the national will. Now then, this whole idea was severely punctured by Hellenism. The old national ties had lost much of their strength; they were absorbed into the vastness of the Empire; the individual man was in limbo: he had lost the guiding orientation of the community.

In times like that, new factors enter the picture. First, men begin to notice that every person is unique. Human character, with its infinite variety, begins to flourish. The arts no longer try to depict ideal models but to capture real-life characters, people of flesh and blood, people who have something unique in their bearing and facial expression. Hellenist sculpture differs from classical Greek sculpture in that it features individual personality.

A second characteristic of this period is a stronger emphasis on personal responsibility and the power of conscience. In former times, a man's moral decisions were automatically conditioned by the national ethos, but now that this ethos was losing its binding force man had to find his own way and act according to his own moral insights. "Morality is no longer a well-defined power, established by authorities; it is subject to the choice of conscience."[27] The conscience needs to be formed and nurtured, so naturally people search for sound rules to navigate life. When the old national religions lost their authority,

[27] Wendland, *Die hellenistisch-römische Kultur*, p. 47. See also A. M. Brouwer, *Paulus de Apostel*, 2 vols. (Zutphen: Ruys, 1933), pp. 76–77.

men turned to the philosophical schools which at that time vied for pre-eminence.

Moralism

That brings us to a third trait of the Hellenistic Age: moralism, the tendency to debate moral values. The philosophical systems of the day all focused on ethics, with which they wanted to put their claim on human lives. Each system was a message of salvation, of self-redemption. Stoicism had always taught that the truly wise man should withdraw into the shelter of apathy, to avoid pain and anxiety. Man must elevate himself above those things that cause the ordinary person to tremble with joy or sob with grief. The truly wise man has wrested himself free from his passions and is able to cope in quiet resignation with all the vicissitudes of life without betraying any emotions. The heroes of this approach to life may suffer the greatest blows, yet they carry on unaffected, indifferent to the clamorous world around them; they are people who control themselves as a rider controls his horse; their inner peace is not disturbed by anything that comes at them. Gallio, the Corinthian governor that Paul once had dealings with, was a brother of Seneca, one of the greatest moral philosophers of Antiquity. The way Gallio sat there in his judgment seat, unperturbed by the screaming mob that had gathered in the marketplace (Acts 18:12–17)—that is how the truly wise man conducts himself under all circumstances of life, far removed from what can upset an ordinary mortal.

Thus, the roaming preachers in the days of Paul were above all preachers of morality, of the art of living. They were often less concerned to say profound things about the structure of the universe than to draw lines along which human life can flourish. People's lives were uprooted and disoriented and in need of new guidelines. They needed to latch on to new rules, to norms that could provide an anchor at critical moments. Both in Rome and in Greece and the East, numerous morality preachers were at work, trying to win people over to their teachings by means of all kinds of ethical ideals.

Syncretism

No seeker after truth will in the long run be satisfied by a moral philosophy, however profound it may be. A moral code needs to be religiously based if it is to bind the heart in an enduring way. This proved all too true also in the days of Hellenism. There were thinkers who lost themselves in abstract reflections on virtue, but the masses longed for something warmer for the soul and something clear and concrete for the mind. A strong appetite for religion pervaded the world of Hellenism, a musing about God and a search for God.

The trouble was, as we have seen, that the old national religions no longer displayed the power they once had. People had seen too much of the world—had come into contact with too many other nations and too many other gods—to be able to accept out of hand that their traditional gods were the only true gods. The countries of the Middle East, Egypt and Babylon, Persia and Syria, had they not from time immemorial practiced their own religions, and had they not developed all kinds of profound thoughts about the nature of the world, about the mysterious connections between this earth and the supernatural realms? For the first time in history people became interested in what other peoples had said, and they began to compare those religious notions with their own. At times they tended to rate the foreign ideas higher than their own, or they tried to explain their own ideas as a further working out of what had been thought up in other countries. But this comparative study always resulted in feeling compelled to abandon the uniqueness of their own religion. Gradually the conviction grew that all nations had worshiped God each in their own way and had depicted his essence in their own manner. They gave him different names, came up with different stories about him, but surely, was it not the same Being they all had a sense of and bowed to? All those different names given to him in different nations, should one not regard them as ever so many weak and stammering denotations of one and the same all-encompassing divine Being? Thus was born that peculiar religious phenomenon that we are wont to designate as syncretism, a combination or fusion of disparate doctrines—in the language of the day: a *theokrasia* ("god-mixing"), because people had begun to realize that the gods of all nations were simply man-made names and descriptions.

This *theokrasia* was possible because the religions that people encountered were all naturalistic religions. They were oriented to nature and in their deepest essence they were forces of nature, forces that penetrated and filled nature, and therefore also man as a small part of nature. Babylon had had its ancient speculations about the structure of the cosmos, and it had surmised divine forces in that cosmos; Babel's gods were nature gods. Egypt very early on had formulated profound myths about mysterious events in nature and about the genesis of life; Egypt's gods were at bottom forces of nature that inhabit everything that exists.

Similarly, all the religions of the Ancient Near East can be seen as naturalistic religions. The gods of Greece, too, were ultimately nothing more than personified forces of nature, even though the powerful imagination of the Greeks had conceived them more as humanlike personalities and given them greater relief.

Naturalistic religions never have absolute contrasts, for nature reconciles all apparent contrasts into a harmonious unity. Nor do these religions have a place for revelation in the biblical sense of the word, for they look upon the entire universe as one continuous revelation and manifestation of God. *Theokrasia* can grow and flourish on the soil of naturalistic religions, because all those names of gods indicate natural phenomena and, with some adjustments, are comparable and interchangeable.[28]

Thus, the Hellenistic Age was pervaded with a syncretistic mood. Not that the religious implications were always realized and acknowledged everywhere, but it does mean that there was a general openness to the religious ideas of other nations. The gods of the East were preached and acknowledged in Greece and Rome, in the belief that basically they did not differ from the gods they had formerly worshiped. Even in regions where the old national culture had remained intact, a measure of tolerance prevailed with respect to other religions. Have not all religions sprung from the same root? Is there not one single universal religious sense in the human heart that simply manifests itself in all existing religions? And do we not all bow before the same mysterious divine being which transcends all thought, which we suspect surrounds us on all sides but which escapes our conceptualization? "*God is near you, he is with you, he is within you.*"[29] These words of Seneca capture the general sense pervading the entire world of that time.

It is exceedingly interesting to find out how the Hellenistic world reacted to the Jews. The Jewish religion was not naturalistic, did not spring from any veneration of the forces of nature, but from the outset had a totally different character. A strictly monotheistic religion, it proclaimed the existence of *one* god, a god who must not be identified with nature or with any force in nature, but a god, rather, who created out of nothing the world and all that is in it. Thus the

---

[28] Cf. H. Kraemer, *De wortelen van het syncretisme* (The Hague, 1937), p. 23 [Cf. Hendrik Kraemer, "Syncretism as a Religious and Missionary Problem," *International Review of Missions* 43.3 (1954): 253–273.].

[29] Seneca, *Epist.* 41.1.

Jewish religion in no way could be a participant in the game of musical chairs involving *theokrasia*. It was different from all other religions and could not possibly acknowledge and tolerate those others.

Hellenistic authors repeatedly discussed the enigma of the Jews. Some Greeks, like Megasthenes and Clearchus of Soli, believed they owed their view of god to India and had borrowed it from the philosophical theories of the Brahmin.[30] The Roman historian Livy expressed surprise at Jewish unwillingness to pronounce the name of their god and the absence in their temple of an image of their god.[31] The Jewish sabbath observance was found offensive, as was their ritual of circumcision, their lack of images, and the emptiness of their sanctuary. The Jewish god was called "obscure." All sorts of tales were invented to show that the Jews borrowed many of their customs from the Egyptians. Later, it was acknowledged that the Jews were not wrong in teaching that the god who upholds all things is himself invisible, and people even developed a certain respect for the strictness and privacy of Jewish religious usages. It is evident from all this, however, that the writers of those days failed to recognize the utter uniqueness of the people of Israel. Their recalcitrance irritated them when they refused to identify their god with the gods that other nations worshiped, but these critics failed to understand that this was impossible since the God that was venerated by Israel and had revealed himself to Israel was entirely different from the gods around them. We should add, however, that the Jews themselves did not always draw the boundary lines clearly either. In a letter written by a Jewish author in the second century B.C., the God of Israel is equated with the all-seeing Zeus—evidence that some Jews were also swept along by the syncretistic mood of the time.

Mysticism

Common to all religious currents of the time was the desire for deliverance and redemption. Stoic philosophers devised beautiful systems of morality, and Neoplatonist thinkers elaborated profound worldviews, but both came up short when it was a matter of delivering man from the misery that he was trapped in. Especially in later times the multitudes were overtaken by a deep yearning to be freed from the bonds of decay. This yearning automatically led to all kinds of

---

[30] O. Holzmann, *Neutestamentliche Zeitgeschichte* (Tübingen: Mohr, 1906), p. 244.

[31] See Eduard Norden, *Agnostos Theos* (Stuttgart: Teubner, 1913), p. 60.

mystery religions which strove after the deification of man through solemn ceremonies and cultic practices, and which formed secret societies with initiation rites that included bathings and similar rituals. This indicated in a symbolic way that new members died in order to rise again to a new life in communion with the deity. Nighttime gatherings gave these forms of religious fellowship a special consecration and solemnity.[32]

It was especially from the eastern provinces that mystery religions entered the western provinces of the Empire. They were embraced by many thousands of converts. Sober moral teachings had not been able to renew life; fresh power was expected from these mystery cults. The mystical initiation gave access to the mysteries of the deity and made a person partake of the divine life and brought him into the most intimate relationship, as it were, with the deity himself or herself. Whoever had received this gift had escaped the power of death; henceforth he went through life as one who had been translated from this dark and dreary world into a world of light and life.

Note that redemption itself was expected from sacral acts. Neither the ascetic regime to which catechumens had to submit prior to the consecration, nor the recondite knowledge they would afterwards receive,[33] but the mystical consecration itself as represented in the symbolic rites made a person partake in the deity and in the renewal of life that issued forth from that deity.[34]

A certain Lucius has left us an elaborate description of the rituals he had to undergo before he was allowed to enter the full light. He first had to spend time in the temple of the Egyptian goddess Isis, until he had a dream in which he was given the assurance that the goddess beckoned him and pronounced him worthy of life. He then came under the direct supervision of a priest who carefully initiated him into the secrets of the cult. After having undergone a number of

---

[32] On mystery religions, see Franz Cumont, *Les religions orientales dans le paganisme romain* (Paris: Leroux, 1907) [Eng. trans., *The Oriental Religions in Roman Paganism* (Norderstedt: Books on Demand, 2019)]; and also Richard Reitzenstein, *Die hellenistische Mysterien-religionen, ihre Grundgedanken und Wirkungen* 2nd ed. (Leipzig: Teubner, 1920).

[33] [Cf. K. J. Popma, *Gospel and History* (Aalten: WordBridge, 2021), pp. 37–38, where literary allusions to rituals in mystery cults are detected in 2 Peter 1:16–19.]

[34] See Reitzenstein, *Mysterienreligionen*, pp. 25ff. Cf. also J. Hoek, *De sacramenten bij Paulus en de Hellenistische mysterie-religies* (diss. Free University; Zutphen: Nauta, 1925), pp. 58ff.

ceremonial acts, he had to fast for ten days and only then was allowed to enter the inner sanctum and participate in a grand encounter with the celestial powers. He came near the brink of death but then received the secret of the true life. He was adopted by Isis and made a partaker of the divine being.

Next to the Isis mysteries there was the cult of Mithras that came from Persia. This mystery cult had a macho character; it summoned a person to intense struggle and total exertion. It gained many adherents among soldiers, who spread it throughout the Roman Empire. Traces of Mithraism are found as far away as the British Isles. Because it had a rite of baptism and also celebrated a mystical meal that expressed unity with the deity, it resembled in some respects the Christian religion with its two sacraments. The apologist Justin Martyr (2nd century A.D.) explains that the devils had imitated the custom of a sacred meal, which was then introduced into Mithraism. He also mentions that the meal was celebrated with bread and cup, accompanied by solemn incantations.[35] Origen too mentions the Mithras cult and relates something of its secrets.[36] Its adherents would meet in close-knit circles and gather in grottoes, sometimes deep underground.

It is also a characteristic feature of mysticism that it attaches great value to the divine element in man. The ancient Greeks had already taught that the human soul is host to a *daimōn*, a divine core that is destined to return to the community of the immortals.[37] This daimonic core, this divine element comes to extraordinary manifestation in the great heroes of mankind: the sublime poets and deep thinkers, the successful kings and victorious generals—they stand closer to the heavenly realm than ordinary mortals. When Alexander the Great in a short time brought world empires to their knees, it was only natural that thousands of his contemporaries began to see him as the son of a god who was guided and borne up by mysterious forces; and Alexander himself was not unwilling to accept this homage. Particularly in the Orient, where it had been believed from time immemorial that kings descended from the gods and therefore deserved to be venerated as gods, the desire was strong to pay divine homage to the magnates and moguls of the earth. But this desire did not remain

---

[35] Justin Martyr, *Apologia*, I, 66.

[36] Origen, *Contra Celsum*, vi.22.

[37] See Paul Wendland, *Die hellenistisch-römische Kultur*, p. 123.

confined to the East; it found so many points of contact in Greek thought and sentiment that there, too, the tendency toward deification gained ground.

Accordingly, when the first emperor of Rome, Caesar Augustus, conquered the world and established peace, he was hailed on all sides as a divine ruler, an incarnation of the deity. People called him *Sōtēr,* the Saviour of the world. They were convinced that in him a new age, an age of prosperity and blessing, had descended upon the world and that the gods had stooped down to mankind. While such an emperor was honored as divine already in his lifetime, after his death he was deemed to have ascended directly to the world of the gods. His daimon, his spirit, detached itself from his body and rose upwards to the blessed regions of the immortals.[38] Thus, a clearly visible thread runs through that whole period, the growing belief that supra-terrestrial powers dwell in mortal men, in emperors and heroes, who for that reason can claim deep reverence and absolute obedience.

It is not difficult to establish that there is an intimate connection between this deification of heroic figures and the above-mentioned inclination to acknowledge and revere great personalities. Thus, not just emperors were deemed worthy of divine homage, but also teachers, priests, poets, thinkers—in short, a whole host of people were honored and venerated as being filled with divine forces. The age of Hellenism was an age in which it was widely felt that the boundary between the human and the divine cannot be sharply drawn, that these two domains seem everywhere to blend into each other.

While the mood of pantheistic mysticism, which hung like a fog over the whole period of Hellenism, on the one hand led to deification of great personalities, and on the other hand was closely related to feelings that bordered on fatalism, on an overwhelming sense of insignificance and imprisonment. This marvelous universe, suffused by divine powers, is ruled from age to age, from generation to generation, with iron necessity. Events in the celestial spheres, the mysterious, unpredictable, and inestimable influences of the intermediate beings that hover as it were between the divine realms and this earth, the revolutions of the heavenly bodies, the wars and tensions in the human world—they are all connected by invisible threads. The world in which we live is laden with riddles; at work in it is a hidden mechanism which props up and propels all

---

[38] Ibid., pp. 149ff.

things and ties everything together. And surrounded by all these movements and stirrings of mysterious forces stands puny man who may have part in divine being yet who is propelled and driven, who at every step is aware that all kinds of supernatural forces are encroaching upon his life, pushing him in a direction where he does not want to go. In his childlike ignorance he does not yet understand the rhythm of cosmic events; he does not see through the subtle connections that bind his existence to beings of an entirely different order, and that is why he plods on with bent shoulders and bowed head. Only a few there are who have begun to understand something of the secret language that is able to determine from the course of the stars what transpires on the earth, who have some inkling of the cadence that governs everything that moves. They are the lucky ones, the seers among the blind, the helpers amid the helpless, the priests among the earth-bound creatures.

The centuries of Hellenism were centuries of powerful historic events. New worlds were discovered, foreign peoples were subjugated, new peoples streamed into ancient regions. It was an age fraught with cataclysms and earthshaking events. In times like that, man realizes more keenly than at any other time his precarious place in the world. He knows he is caught between the stirrings and struggles of dynamic forces that are infinitely stronger than he is. And this knowledge makes him anxious and cautious, unsure of himself and fearful of what might happen to him. All this suffused the age and explains that fierce longing for redemption, that lethargy and weariness, that superstitious belief in astrology, that shuddering before man's very existence.

Twilight

As we survey this whole period, we can do no better than to characterize it as a time of twilight and dusk. An old world, molding and crumbling, was going under. Was the sun setting and night falling, or was the world being prepared for the rise of a new dawn? Expectations ran high. People spoke of a new age, of the *pax Romana*, an everlasting realm of peace under the blessed reign of Roman emperors. But were those expectations truly rooted in a hopeful heart, or was there something forced and artificial about them? Were those anticipations at bottom no more than pumped-up self-flattery rather than innermost conviction?

One thing is certain, and that is that the period in which Paul went out into the world distinguished itself in many respects from the ordinary situation in the history of nations. Throughout the ages the world has seen national communities with bonds that were wrapped in religious convictions, communities that were focused on the worship of national gods, that were carried by a host of national ideas and national customs, and that were devoted to the veneration of national leaders and kings. The old Greek polis was a national community, albeit that it could flourish only at the local level. The Ancient Near East knew national religions with distinct gods, and in those religions it carried on its own form of life for many centuries. But what is thoroughly new and revolutionary in the days of Paul was that these national communities were being absorbed into the world-embracing community of the Empire, that the national religions lost their supports and began to mingle in a hopeless mixture of vague, common religiosity. For the first time in history the concept of humanity entered people's thoughts and feelings—humanity, not in the sense of a community of communities, one that embraced all nations, all peoples and all ethnic groups, but humanity in the sense of the world-wide unity of nation-less beings, of wanderers without a country, of uprooted, groping and seeking souls. This concept of humanity took shape in an Empire in which all things human, both Eastern and Western, were meant to feel at home.

Indeed, it was no normal world that Paul engaged in a mighty struggle. On all his journeys the great apostle encountered the spiritual powers that dominated the world of his day. In the interior he collided with remnants of the old forms of worship, of what remained of the ancient folk religions. In the cities he competed with moralizing philosophers, with Stoics who recommended with ardent conviction their *apatheia*, their inner freedom from emotions, as the only remedy against the cares and worries of life. Paul collided with teachers of mysticism, people who claimed to know something of the music of the spheres, of the secrets concealed in events, people who were revered as divine teachers to whose leadership one could entrust oneself if one were to be safe when passing through the muddle of daily events. They alone were able to disclose the secret of the stars, of the intermediate beings, of the spirits that determine the life of man on earth. They alone were able to point out the paths that were secure. Here flourished the mystery religions with their rich symbolic rituals, their nightly séances, their sacramental consecrations, their promise that they could ensure mortal man's participation in the eternal, immortal life of the gods. Here were erected the altars for worshiping Caesar, the embodiment of divine power, the symbol of the unity of the human race, the community of the nations. Paul had to forge a way through all these currents and emotions, to bring the message of that other realm, the kingdom of Jesus Christ, the Son of God, the true Redeemer, the Saviour of the world. He was to preach the new life, the life of faith in His atonement for our sins, whereby alone mortal man can inherit immortality.

Countless impediments which continually hamper our own missionary work were unknown to the apostle, at least not to that agree. Unlike us, he did not have to struggle with difficult languages, in which every word must be captured as it were with great effort if it is to be serviceable as a vehicle for the gospel. Wherever he went, Paul could speak in Greek, and this Greek language, owing to the labour of the rabbis and owing especially to the translation of the Old Testament, the Septuagint, was a ready means to transmit and give voice to the new message. Paul did not have to deal with staunch ethnic communities, strong tribal loyalties that offered tough resistance to anything that was felt to be a violation of their integrity. The nations he visited were all involved in a process of erosion and dissolution; their religions had shriveled up, eaten away by skepticism, overgrown by philosophical reasonings, hollowed out by notions from abroad. Paul did not need to tackle the kind of antipathy that arises among every vibrant people whenever it is stalked by preachers of other gods and other doctrines; on the contrary, in Paul's day there were numerous preachers, from both East and West, who traveled from city to city, where people were always ready and eager to hear what they had to say. In short, many factors that confront our modern missions with major problems had been removed, as it were, even before the apostle of the Gentiles began to travel the military roads of the Empire with the gospel of the Cross.

It would be folly, however, to think that Paul toured the world on smooth paths. He was forced to deal with challenges other than ours, and those challenges were not smaller in size or lighter in weight. When he arrived somewhere he would have a willing audience, but people were all too quick to absorb his words into a cluster of vague religious notions they had carefully formed for themselves. How was Paul to make clear that what he proclaimed was totally different from what they thought and taught? How could he explain to them that when he talked about moderation and justice, his teaching had nothing to do with the moralizing sermons of itinerant Stoics? How could he distance himself from *theokrasia*, the powerful suction of syncretism? How could he make clear to those pampered ears that Jesus is not an incarnation of the deity that dwells in every man, nor the unveiling of cosmic secrets, but that He is the only Saviour of the world? To sum up, how could he face the world of that time and preach to that world, in the language of the day, the one and eternal gospel, and do so in such a way that it would captivate the hearts and yet in no way be made of none effect through misunderstanding?

It was no easy task facing the apostle. No doubt his time also had much in common with ours, yet it differed in structure and orientation. In our days, too, the old religions are languishing on the mission field, inundated as they are by the inroads of western science. But that science, which today has its uprooting effect around the world, is different from the science of the days of the apostles. It is less fraught with mysticism, less riding on disbelief and superstition, less accommodating of notions nurtured in the older religions, less focused on the inner redemption of people, less filled with views about divine powers in the universe. Our science is more sober, and infinitely more materialistic, a-religious, more rational, but also more cruel, crass, and disruptive. In addition, the reaction of peoples is different than in Paul's days, when the mysterious fluidity of the Hellenistic mind loosened and dissolved the old religions into a new, a-national, all-inclusive doctrine of salvation. In our time, the penetration of western science and technology is everywhere awakening strong reactions from the nations, whose religions are taking a stance against them, abandoning what is no longer tenable, yet stubbornly defending every inch of the national heritage. They are all swept along in the maelstrom of the mighty events of our time; they live in a feverish frenzy; sometimes they are delirious from being mentally unhinged. And yet they will not surrender their ancient rights. Our world and the world of Paul are equally caught up in an enormous crisis of thought and of life, but the symptoms are different; the disease has a different cause and expresses itself differently. Our time also lacks a concept of world empire, a concept of a nationless humanity, of an all-encompassing community that once inspired the thinkers and poets of Antiquity.

When we sum it all up, it cannot escape us that the chances for a rapid spread of the gospel was infinitely more favorable in Paul's days than they are today.

Through his preparatory grace God had opened the world so that the message of Jesus Christ might complete its swift course. The exchange of intellectual and spiritual goods was far more intense than at present; there were far more opportunities for the spontaneous distribution of the word of truth. That old world had many channels the gospel could utilize. The world of today is harder, harsher, tougher. The contrast between East and West, which at that time seemed for a short while to be fading, today frustrates all our efforts, like a stubborn reality. There is much less willingness to listen, to exchange ideas; there is more grim unbelief, angry antipathy, bitter mockery. The gospel of Christ is less able to be a message for the world because it is reproached for belonging to the exports of Western culture, of the culture that has proved itself a master at manufacturing instruments of killing. Despite the apparent likeness, everything is different now than before, which cannot but strike anyone who compares the world of Paul's days with the perplexing revolution that we witness today in the mentality of the nations on the mission field.

There is one thing, however, that we must not lose sight of as we contemplate the change. Then as now, the gospel is not "*after man*" (Gal. 1:11). In those days the gospel contradicted man's longings; in our time the gospel does not affirm the desires of the nations where it is preached. In the days of our apostle the gospel was a stumbling block to the Jews and, ultimately, foolishness to the Greeks (1 Cor. 1:23), despite the latter's sympathy and willingness to listen. It is the same today for the Hindus and the Japanese, for the natives of Africa and the peoples of the Dutch East Indies. The gospel may seem to have better opportunities at certain times; it may spread more quickly at one time than at other times; nevertheless, to every proud human heart it remains foolishness and madness. Its passage through world history is a *via dolorosa,* a path of sorrows. What is spoken by the evangelist is spoken against by all the nations of mankind. When Paul thinks about the enigma of all these things, he writes: "*For it is written, I will destroy the wisdom of the wise, and will bring to nothing the understanding of the prudent . . . because the foolishness of God is wiser than men*" (1 Cor. 1:19, 25).

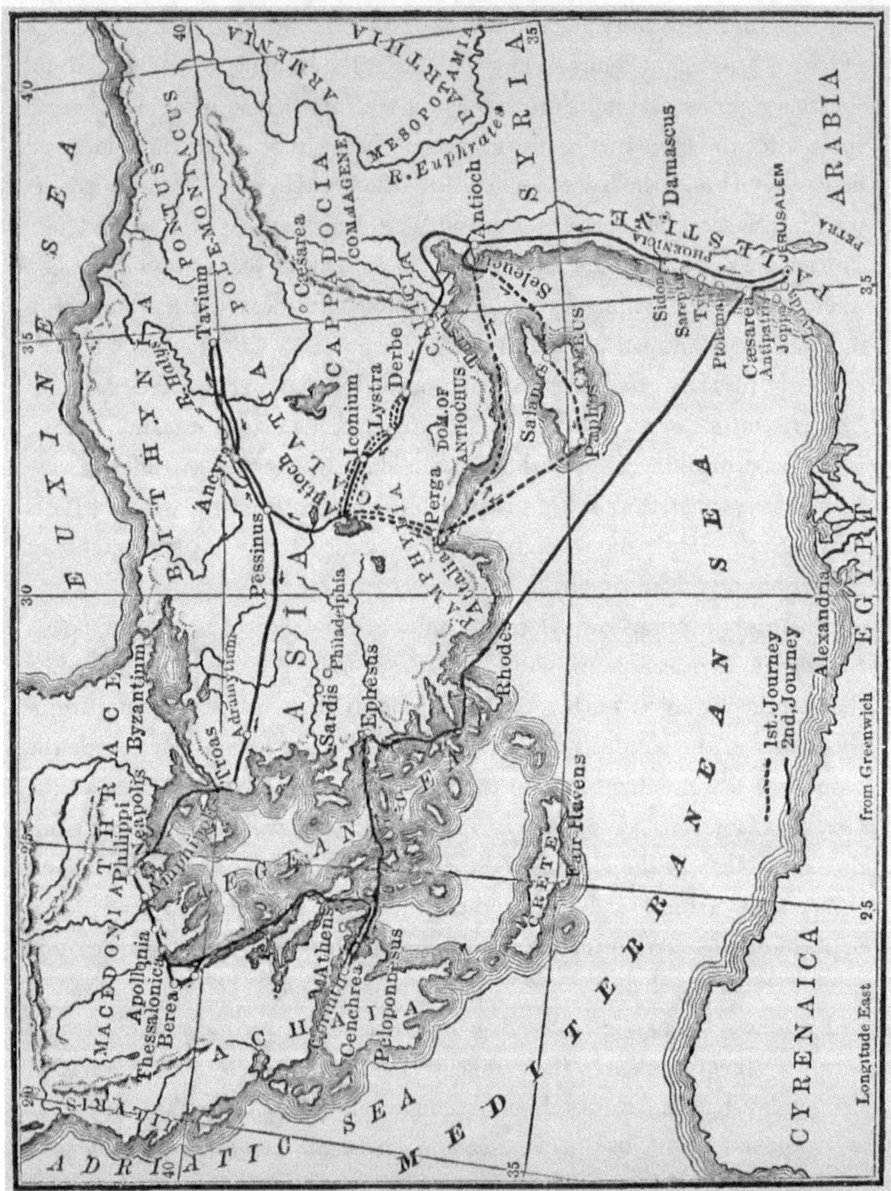

Maps of Paul's missionary travels

Source: Rev. Lyman Abbot, *An Illustrated Commentary on the Acts of the Apostles,* vol. IV (New York, Chicago, and New Orleans: A. S. Barnes & Co., 1878).

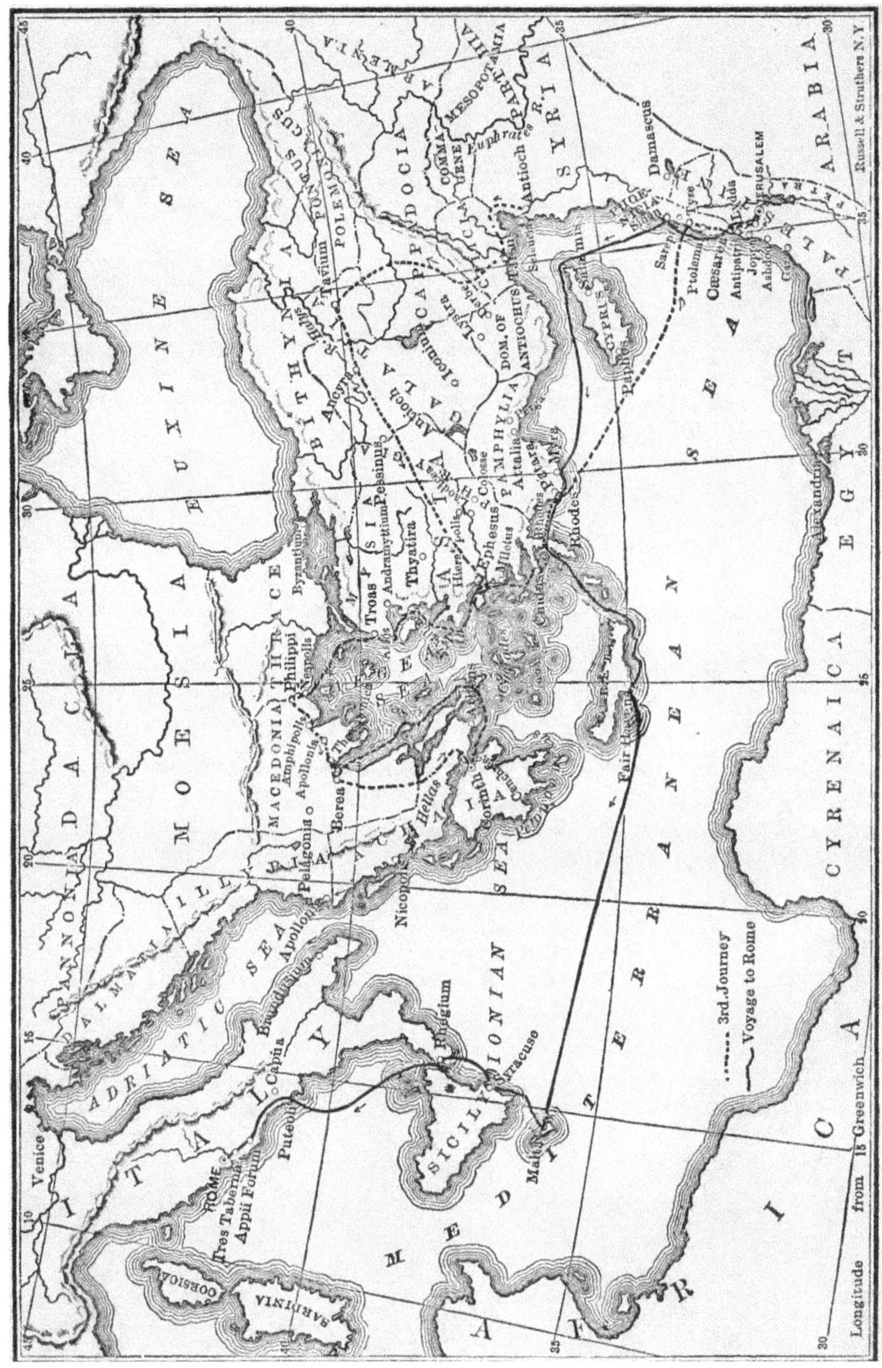

EUXINE SEA
MOESIA
DACIA
THRACE
MACEDONIA
BITHYNIA
GALATIA
CAPPADOCIA
PONTUS
ASIA
PAMPHYLIA
CYPRUS
SYRIA
ARABIA
EGYPT
CYRENAICA
AFRICA
ITALY
SICILY
SARDINIA
CORSICA
ADRIATIC SEA
IONIAN SEA
MEDITERRANEAN SEA
Damascus
Antioch
Ephesus
Miletus
Rhodes
Troas
Philippi
Neapolis
Amphipolis
Apollonia
Berea
Corinth
Athens
Nicopolis
Rome
Appii Forum
Tres Tabernæ
Puteoli
Capua
Rhegium
Syracuse
Melita
Fair Havens
Alexandria
Jerusalem
Cæsarea
Ptolemais
Tyre
Sidon
Paphos
Salamis
Perga
Attalia
Iconium
Lystra
Derbe
Tarsus
Ancyra
Pessinus
Thyatira
Byzantium
Venice
Euphrates R.
3rd. Journey
Voyage to Rome
Longitude from Greenwich
Russell & Struthers N.Y.

4. Preaching the Gospel on the Mission Field

What Paul himself says about it

Paul and his aides preached the gospel of Christ as itinerant preachers in the world of the Roman Empire. Naturally, we who are called to do the same in the no less turbulent world of our own day and age are extremely interested in learning how the great apostle acquainted the people of his day and age with the message of the Saviour. How did he approach them; through what portals did he penetrate the fortresses of paganism? Which aspects of the gospel did he bring into prominence? How did Paul manage to keep the attention of his audience? How did he impress them with the majesty of the Word of God? These are all questions that deserve to be considered one by one.

The apostle himself has told us something of his preaching on the mission field in a few of his letters. He gives us glimpses of how he went about it and what he emphasized. And then we notice very quickly that he was thoroughly familiar with what lived in the hearts of his hearers. He was fully abreast of Judaism, having been born and raised in it. But paganism, too, was an open book for him; already as a boy he must have observed pagan life as it unfolded in Tarsus, and in later years he encountered that pagan life on every one of his travels. In the opening chapter of his letter to the Romans, Paul gives a moving overview of the spiritual and moral bankruptcy of his day; he shows how dishonoring God had made the pagan world more and more impotent in its battle against carnal passions, and how physical lust was progressing from decadence to decadence. The picture he paints there is indeed very dark and is evidence that this ambassador of Jesus Christ, as he traveled through the cities of Asia Minor and Greece, did not allow himself to be blinded by the splendor of marble and gold, but saw through the utter vanity of paganism.

Let us examine more closely for a moment a few of the places where Paul talks about his preaching among the pagans.

I am thinking first of all of what the apostle writes in 1 Thessalonians 1:9–10. There he describes the impression that the conversion of the Thessalonians made on the believers in the neighbouring regions. *"For they themselves report concerning us the kind of reception we had among you, and how you turned to God from idols to serve the living and true God, and to wait for his Son from heaven, whom he raised from the dead, Jesus who delivers us from the wrath to come."* Strictly speaking, the passage talks only about the conversion of the Thessalonians, but we have reason to believe that this brief summary is at the same time a resumé of the apostle's teaching in Thessalonica. Let me already note in passing that this resumé in the main agrees with what we learn from the Book of Acts about the content of Paul's preaching on the mission field.

We are immediately struck by several features of this passage. First, conversion is described as a "turning to God from idols," as a turning to "the living and true God." These words closely resemble all sorts of expressions in the Old Testament. Take, for example, the passage in which the prophet confidently proclaims, against the vanities of the pagans, that *"the Lord is the true God; he is the living God and the everlasting King"* (Jer. 10:10). This passage, too, portrays the pagans in particular as worshipers of imaginary, self-made gods, gods who are not "living," gods you could never have a relationship with because the people who imagined them and then made images of them in gold and silver will always, to a greater or lesser extent, feel elevated above these gods. Creative man, the craftsman and the goldsmith, can always take leave of his imagined god; he can forget about him, and he can destroy his image. Conversion, by contrast, is always a turning away from the idols and a turning to "the living and true God."

A second feature that strikes us in this word from the apostle is what we might call the eschatological nature of the preaching of Christ. We will come across this eschatological nature more than once in another context as well, for it is one of the hallmarks of Pauline preaching among the pagans.[39] What we understand by it is that Paul, when he preaches Christ in a pagan environment, starts with the *eschaton*, with the second coming of Christ in the last days, at the end of the age. He does not yet speak of the Cross of atonement, nor does he start with an extensive account of the life and work of Jesus Christ. No, he begins with the awe-inspiring message that someday Christ shall come to judge—to judge the living and the dead. And only in connection with that future expectation does he mention the resurrection—the message of Christ's rising from

---

[39] See my *Christusprediking in de volkerenwereld* (Kampen: Kok, 1939), p. 8 [Eng. trans. in *The J. H. Bavinck Reader*, pp. 110–142, at 113f.].

the dead. The resurrection then is the proof that God has called Christ to bring all people into judgment. Note that the background of the resurrection, the Cross that redeems the world, is not mentioned first. Initially, the entire work of atonement remains unmentioned: the spotlight falls on the end times.

Thus, first to be mentioned in Paul's preaching on the mission field is Christ as Judge of the World. Only then comes a brief indication of the work of atonement: "*who delivers us from the wrath to come.*" That deliverance, too, is presented in an eschatological light: it is the coming wrath that causes one to long for deliverance. And deliverance is the wonderful gift of the same Christ whom one day we will face as Judge.

Such, in brief, is the line of thought Paul presents in his first letter to the Thessalonians. It is probably also the line he preferred to follow on the mission field. There he would first talk about God, the living God in contrast to the idols. Then he would call people to repent and turn to the true worship of God. He would then segue to the Last Judgment that was coming, and in that connection would mention Christ as the coming Judge. After mentioning that name, he would talk about the resurrection of Christ as the sign that God had truly appointed Him to be the Judge of the living and the dead. And only after this would he indicate in a few sober words the deliverance that is granted us by the same Christ. This basic pattern can be captured as follows: God—repentance and conversion—judgment—Christ—resurrection—salvation. The pattern can easily be seen in his address in Lystra as well as in his speech on Mars Hill.

A second passage in which Paul speaks in his letters about the content of his message on the mission field is found in 1 Corinthians 2:1–2: "*And I, when I came to you, brothers, did not come proclaiming to you the testimony of God with lofty speech or wisdom. For I decided to know nothing among you except Jesus Christ and him crucified.*" Some commentators have tried to read these words of Paul as if he had deliberately decided not to give a "testimony of God" in Corinth, but instead to confine himself to proclaiming the crucified Christ. In his evocative book *The Christ of the Indian Road*, the noted missionary Stanley Jones writes that in Athens Paul spoke far too much about God and that is why the speech on Mars Hill was a failure; he was deliberately silent about the Cross and instead reasoned extensively about the greatness and omnipresence of God.

"This studied omission of the Cross is the secret of his comparative failure at Athens and his subsequent change at Corinth."[40]

I find it impossible to agree with this comment. It creates a contrast where there is none. Leaving aside the question whether the speech on Mars Hill can be called a "failure,"[41] it seems to me quite mistaken to suggest that on the relatively short journey from Athens to Corinth Paul was converted from Theology to Christology, from the "testimony of God" to the Crucified One. The words "*the testimony of God*" can be read in two ways: as "the testimony that comes to us from God," or as "the testimony about God." The first reading is probably more correct, but even if one leans toward the second, there is not a shred of contrast between the testimony of God and the proclamation of the crucified Christ. The testimony of God is precisely the Cross; when we are talking about God we are talking about the Cross; the Cross is the content of the testimony of God. In no way does Paul wish to indicate that in Corinth he wanted to follow a different path than he had in Athens. He is only emphasizing that he did not bring "the testimony of God" (i.e., the message of the Crucified One) "*with lofty speech or wisdom*,"[42] but rather in its dramatic gravity and childlike simplicity.

Now one may observe that in Athens, Paul undeniably did not talk about the Cross at all, did not even mention it, and therefore there is a contrast between what he did in Athens and what he chose to do in Corinth. This objection seems valid, but it does not do justice to the fact that Paul's speech in Athens was broken off at an unfavorable moment. Paul had talked about the coming Judgment; he had also already mentioned the fact of the Resurrection. All that remained was for him to explain how the same risen Christ "*delivers us from the wrath to come.*" This last part of his speech was lost in the muttering of his hearers. His first sermon in Athens indeed did not give the apostle the opportunity to illuminate the full truth about the Cross, and we can be certain that he

---

[40] E. Stanley Jones, *The Christ of the Indian Road* (London: Hodder and Stoughton, 1926), p. 26 [quoting H. R. Mackintosh, *The Originality of the Christian Message* (New York: Scribner, 1920)].

[41] See next chapter.

[42] [Cf.: "with excellency of speech or of wisdom" (KJV); "with eloquence of human wisdom" (NIV); "with big words and great learning" (Good News); "with polished speeches and the latest philosophy" (Message); "not in gloriousnes of wordes or of wysdome" (Tyndale).]

regretted it deeply. But that does not give us the right to say that in Athens Paul remained silent about the Cross, let alone to say that he did so deliberately. In Corinth, too, there is no doubt that when he addressed the pagans there, Paul did not choose the message of the Cross as his point of departure, for the simple reason that it would have made no sense to his hearers. To preach the Cross to a pagan audience one must first speak about God and about the judgment of God. In the absence of a warning about a coming judgment, the Cross is no more than a story about an incomprehensible and meaningless event. The Cross does not acquire its depth and power until we see it against the backdrop of God's judgment. Paul would not have wanted his message in Corinth to be any different from the one in Athens, but he does give us deeper insight into his aim. In all his preaching his chief concern was the Cross. The Cross could not be the point of departure for his message, but it was the center, the core of all his words. The sober words about it in his letter to the Corinthians is proof positive that neither in Athens nor anywhere else had he wanted to preach anything other than the testimony of God, namely, the message of Jesus Christ, the Crucified One.

This conclusion is fully in line with another word of the apostle that is found in 2 Corinthians 5:20: "*We are therefore ambassadors for Christ, God making his appeal through us. We implore you on behalf of Christ, be reconciled to God.*" These words are a wonderful sign of an apostle's self-confidence. Paul is very sure of himself as an ambassador of Christ the King. The core content of his preaching is defined once again as the proclamation of reconciliation with God, through the Cross.

Looking again at these texts, we realize that one must distinguish between the passages where the apostle summarizes the central thrust of his preaching on the mission field and the passages where he gives insight into the structure of his preaching. His summarizing statements indicate irrefutably that no matter where he came Paul wanted to be nothing but a preacher of the Cross, even if he was fully cognizant of the fact that such preaching was "*a stumbling block to Jews and folly to Gentiles*" (1 Cor. 1:23). In the other passages he shows how carefully he constructed his message in direct relation to his audience.

What is easily discernible in Paul's letters is that he experienced the task of preaching Christ as an arduous one. Not that he was ashamed of it.[43] On the contrary, he spoke freely and boldly what he had to say. But at every turn he was aware how extremely difficult it is to convey the unsearchable riches of the love of Christ to people who do not know what sin is and what it means to be lost. In the letter to the Colossians Paul asks the church to pray for his work, "*that God may open a door to us for the word, to declare the mystery of Christ*" (Col. 4:3). To declare a mystery is no easy task; it demands a lot of love for our audience. It can seem sometimes that we are standing before a solid wall, a wall we cannot penetrate, a wall that just bounces our words back to us. Another time it is as if a door opens, and we clearly see the path we are to follow for proclaiming the gospel in such a way that the people understand the seriousness of it and heed the call. That this experienced missionary commends himself to a church with a request for prayer on his behalf is eloquent evidence of his humility.

Preaching the gospel in Lystra

Having heard Paul's own testimony from his letters, we do well to turn to the Book of Acts to see what it teaches us about the apostle's preaching.

Luke has recorded two extensive speeches of Paul, one that he held in Antioch of Pisidia, another that he delivered in Athens. The first speech was given in a synagogue on a sabbath day (Acts 13:16–41). Its salutation is: "*Men of Israel and you who fear God.*" This shows clearly that it is addressed to Jews and God-fearers, the proselytes. Accordingly, it contains many references to the Old Testament. Like the speech that Stephen held in his defence as recorded in Acts 7, Paul's speech on this occasion gives a bird's eye view of the history of the people of God and shows how that history has been fulfilled in the coming of the Messiah. Since we wish to focus right now on his preaching among the pagans, we shall not go into the speech in Antioch at this time. There remains the speech in Athens; more about that one later.

In addition to these two longer speeches, Luke has also reported on a few shorter addresses, given on various occasions. We ought to pay attention to these

---

[43] ["*I am not ashamed of the gospel,*" Paul assured the believers in Rome, "*for it is the power of God for salvation to everyone who believes, to the Jew first and also to the Greek*" (Rom. 1:16).]

as well if we want to gain an accurate picture of how Paul used to preach. The first of these short addresses was held in Lystra, on the first missionary journey.

In Acts chapter 14 Luke has left us a vivid picture of the setting. There is a man in Lystra who is lame from birth and has never been able to walk. While preaching the gospel in the market square in the center of town, Paul notices that this man has the faith to be healed, so he breaks off his speech, looks straight at him, and in a loud voice says to him: "On your feet! Stand up!" Instantly the man jumps up and starts walking around. This startling miracle causes a mighty stir among the people gathered there. With great enthusiasm they crowd around Paul and Barnabas and start shouting in their native tongue: "*The gods have come down to us in the likeness of men!*" In their fevered fantasy and heated imagination they identify Barnabas, the older and silent man, with the supreme god Zeus, while identifying Paul with Hermes, the messenger of the gods. In an earlier chapter we noted that in the interior of Lycaonia we come face to face with a traditional strand of paganism that was still very much alive, one that was rooted in the life of the common people. Circulating in that part of Asia Minor were legends, also known from other sources, about manifestations of Zeus and Hermes. Thus it was understandable that the people interpreted the miracle as evidence of Paul's divinity.

Meanwhile, the priest of the Zeus temple has gone into action. He soon arrives in the square with a team of sacrificial bulls decorated with garlands. He is swarmed by a mass of people, all eager to offer a solemn sacrifice to the unexpected visitors from the world of the gods. At that moment, Paul intervenes. Evidently, he has not quite understood what the people are planning, but no sooner does he spot the decorated bulls than he realizes what the intention is. He and Barnabas rush into the crowd and as soon as the crowd quiets down the apostle begins to speak. His talk obviously is not a prepared speech but an impromptu protest against what is going on. That is why this speech in Lystra packs such a punch, pressed as it is from a distressed heart, fired with hot indignation at all this pagan foolishness.

> [15] Men, why are doing these things? We also are men, of like nature with you, and we bring you good news, that you should turn from these vain things to a living God, who made the heaven and the earth and the sea and all that is in them.

> [16] In past generations he allowed all the nations to walk in their own ways.
> [17] Yet he did not leave himself without witness, for he did good by giving you rains from heaven and fruitful seasons, satisfying your hearts with food and gladness.

Paul does not mince words: "*Men, why are you doing these things?*" and in the next breath he pulls no punches: "*Turn from these* vain *things!*" Vain indeed, for they are not grounded in the reality of the relation between God and man; it is meaningless and pointless. With a single word, delivered point-blank, Paul captures paganism in its hollowness, because it is blind to the boundary between of God and this world, and as a result it continually deifies man and humanizes God. "We are only human," he reminds them, or literally, "*We also are men, of like nature with you.*" In other words, "We are no different from you, weak human beings, just as frail and insignificant as you are." Words often derive their strength from the situation in which they are spoken. When a man whom a large crowd takes to be a god and who is about to be worshiped as Hermes talks like that about himself and instead of greedily inhaling the homage about to be offered him spurns it as a "vain thing," as hollow vanity, then one can be sure that those words will not have failed to impress the masses.

You must "*turn from these vain things,*" says Paul. Greek has two words for such turning, for conversion: *metanoia* means more a change in thinking, *epistrophē* emphasizes more a change in one's attitude towards life. In Lystra he uses the latter, in Athens the former (Acts 17:30). In Athens there are thinkers who devote themselves to reflection: they need to change their thinking. In Lystra, the pagans are actively doing things: they need to change their attitude. Wherever Paul comes to preach, repentance and conversion is at the forefront. He was fully justified later in saying about his work in Ephesus that he had testified to both Jews and Greeks "*of repentance toward God and of faith in our Lord Jesus Christ*" (Acts 20:21). Here again he stands before us as the preacher of repentance and conversion.

The repentance commanded here becomes very specific when it is defined as "*turning to a living God, who made the heaven and the earth and the sea and all that is in them.*" Once again we are struck by the term "living God," which we also heard in the letter to the Thessalonians. The pagan gods Zeus and Hermes and Apollo and Diana are dead gods, they do not make the heart tremble with dread, they do not fill with fear and angst, they do not cause deep longing for the atonement of guilt, they do not crush pride and lust. One can listen for hours to stories about all those gods, and then smile and walk away and be the same person as before. The gods of the pagans are tales, colorful legends, artful fables, but they have no vital relationship with the sinful heart of man. Man must turn away from them; he is to wrest himself free from all those siren songs and turn to the living God, the God before whom one trembles but in whom one can then also put one's hope.

As Paul continues to preach, he explains the breach that has entered history. "*In past generations he allowed all the nations to walk in their own ways.*" Their own ways—no sharper critique of paganism has ever been made. Pagan religion is man-made, fabricated and fantasized. Humans choose the paths they will walk on, and God, in his inscrutable, seeming indifference, leaves them be. He does not intervene with judgment. He does not cut through all those idle fantasies with the razor-sharp words of prophets.

There you have the riddle of history that fills us with astonishment. Apparently, the living God is a God in the background, a *deus otiosus*, a God at leisure, a God who isn't doing anything. He leaves foolish man alone on his self-chosen ways.

Paul did not finish this thought; his speech appears to have been interrupted. It would seem that he had wanted to say that with the coming of Jesus Christ everything had changed: that God no longer leaves the nations alone but instead calls them to turn and worship Him. From now on, the word of His prophets and apostles must be heard everywhere, in the East and in the West, wherever people have lost their way.

Paul still gets the chance to quickly mention that in those former times God never left the pagans altogether. The fact that here, at the city gate of Lystra, close to the temple of Zeus, the apostle can speak about God—that the Greek language even has a word for God—is strong evidence that "*God did not leave himself without witness.*" In the tremendous contest of world history there has always been a witness that stood up for God, that defended Him against all man's foolish thoughts. That one witness was the work of God himself: "*He did good by giving you rains from heaven and fruitful seasons, satisfying your hearts with food and gladness.*" Those blessings stand in the heart of history as a mighty word from God, as a permanent testimony of his compassion. Nations overwhelmed and slaughtered each other; blood flowed from the earliest days till now; hatred and bitterness turned the world into a hell. Nevertheless, every day the sun rose in its benevolent splendor; fresh green displayed its beauty as if it had no knowledge of all that misery. God's language spoke right through all those centuries of twisted human deeds.

Such in brief was the message that Paul preached in Lystra. He was not able to finish his speech; he wasn't even able to mention the name of Christ. Still, the extract Luke has left us with shows how well constructed the message was. The impression it made must have been critical.[44]

Preaching before the philosophers of Athens

Paul's encounter on Mars Hill occurred on his second missionary journey. Several years therefore separate the two missionary addresses—years filled with experiences and encounters.

The first thing to keep in mind is that the audience Paul addressed in Athens was entirely different from the popular crowd he spoke to in Lystra. In Athens he did not face a throng of common people who lived in old traditions, but instead a group of men of erudition, men who had long thought about the basic questions of philosophy and who knew the doctrines taught by the various schools of the time. They were men without roots, not grounded, men in whom the power of the old pagan teachings had already paled, men who were inclined to poke fun at what the forefathers had held sacred. Such were the men Paul faced in Athens.

One need not have had much experience on the mission field to grasp that the audience in Athens was the most difficult audience an evangelist could ever imagine. These men were brimming with thoughts and ideas; they would pay attention to lessons in philosophy not from a lively interest in truth, but purely from the wish to hear something new. It is easier to impress the first swearing trooper you meet with the majesty of God's Word than these sophisticated consumers of theoretical speculations who are interested only in the structure of the argument and not in God's truth. That Paul, the tentmaker from Tarsus, took the risk of striking up a conversation with such philosophical connoisseurs

---

[44] [Luke ends his account by recording that it "*restrained the people from offering sacrifice*" to Paul and Barnabas, albeit "*scarcely*."]

certainly shows that he was a man who was not afraid to go wherever God wished to send him.

Outwardly, the speech in Athens is of course different from the one held in Lystra. Paul carefully observed the rules of rhetoric and paid attention to mellifluous figures of speech. His very first words are in keeping with the demands of urbane courtesy: "*Men of Athens, I perceive that in every way you are very religious*" (Acts 17:22). No doubt this sounded like praise in their ears, even though Paul did not mean it that way. Then followed the elegant segue into the inscription on the altar TO THE UNKNOWN GOD: "*What you worship as unknown. this I proclaim to you.*" Next, in verse 25, Paul turns poetic by using the rhyming words *zōē* and *pnoē* (God does not need anything, since he himself "*gives to all mankind* life *and* breath *and everything*"). Moving along, in verse 27 he says that "*God is not far from each one of us*"—thus resorting to *litotes*, a figure of speech popular among Greek and Roman writers which ironically emphasizes a special quality by denying its opposite. The entire discourse on the Areopagus thus has the character of a literary composition, a speech well suited for a discriminating audience.

In the present context we do not wish to enter into what I would like to call the Mystery of Mars Hill, which poses at least two questions: *For what reason* and *to what extent* was the apostle linking up with ideas that were well known particularly in Stoic philosophy? That Paul quotes with approval some lines from Greek poets is by itself reason enough for considering this question seriously. We shall therefore discuss it separately in a later chapter. At this point our interest is especially in his line of argument. We see that it shows striking similarity both with what the apostle himself described in his letter to the Thessalonians as well as with what he had said earlier in Lystra. Leaving aside the beginning for a moment, we note that in Athens, too, the apostle took his point of departure in proclaiming the living God, "*the God who made the world and everything in it, being Lord of heaven and earth*" (vs. 24). That said, Paul exposes the vanity of paganism with its man-made temples and its worship of the gods to serve their needs. In Lystra, in response to the situation of the moment, he had spoken of "vain things," but in Athens he spoke in more general terms; yet in both cases the message is the same. God has no need of us and our worship. He is infinitely far above us. Paganism has taken him down, has made him dependent on the devotion of men, whereas in actual fact God is elevated far above our human thoughts and deeds.

This message is then followed by a somewhat longer statement of God's wise sustenance of his creatures and His nearness to the children of man. That particular portion of the discourse is closest to the Hellenistic world of thought. Then, in verse 29, the apostle resumes his line of argument and lays bare the folly of idol worship, followed by the command to repent. In Lystra that command had come first; in that city one of the most vivid acts of paganism, sacrificing to idols, stared him in the face. In Athens the call to repent comes at the end of a well-argued case. In a brief flash, Paul shows the break that has entered history. The "*times of ignorance*"—the times in which God allowed the nations "*to walk in their own ways*" (Lystra)—those times are over. The time has come when the Creator of heaven and earth calls all men to repentance. These words contain a quiet allusion to what was generally believed in those days, namely that a new era, a new period of world history, had commenced—that the old values were gone and new prospects were opening up. Very well, the apostle, too, indicates that the new era has been ushered in, but as chief mark of that new era he points to the command to come to repentance.

From the command to repent Paul moves on to speak of the coming judgment that hangs like a storm cloud over this absurd world. That judgment will be executed by a man whom God has appointed and who for that purpose was raised from the dead. Notice that the proclamation of the Christ, here too, is of an eschatological nature: it is Christ as Judge that is impressed upon the Athenian intellectuals. The Resurrection is sketched less as a sign of the completion of the work of salvation than as the proof that Christ is worthy to stand on the Last Day as the Judge of heaven and earth.

Recalling the pattern that we found in 1 Thessalonians 1:9–10, we can clearly identify the basic pattern of the speech on Mars Hill. Paul's preaching, we saw there, proceeded along the lines of God—repentance and conversion—judgment—Christ—resurrection—salvation. Paul was not able to deal with the last part in Athens, but as for everything else we can see that he stayed true to his old pattern.

Some short passages

Besides these two excerpts of speeches, the Book of Acts contains a myriad of short, isolated passages that inform us of the character of Paul's preaching among the pagans.

I am thinking in the first place of the response to the jailer in Philippi. This word to the jailer has no introduction, no prior explanation of the need to repent or of the coming judgment. It is simply a summons to "*believe in the Lord Jesus*" (Acts 16:31). Such a direct summons was possible in this case because the jailer himself had asked what he must do to be saved. He was a seeker after *sōteria*, salvation. Now, apart from the question what that man himself at that moment understood by salvation, Paul could assure him with one word that salvation is found only in Christ Jesus. The trembling jailer, who already saw judgment descending upon him and who shuddered in the presence of God, could straightway hear the message of salvation. This time God himself had taken care of an introduction. All Paul needed to do was speak the final word, the word he had not had a chance to speak in Athens.

On his third missionary journey Paul stayed some years in Ephesus. We have no record of what he preached there. The only thing we know about it is a brief comment from the mouth of the town clerk. This man in his courageous address to the rioting mob said that Paul and his companions were "neither robbers of temples nor blasphemers of your goddess" (Acts 19:37). This last comment in particular is significant; it indicates that Paul tried to persuade people to repent of those "vain things," yet he never supported his case with grim portrayals of the vanity of pagan gods. He did not start by mocking the legends that circulated about Diana or refuting them one by one as dangerous and false. Instead, he confined himself to a few remarks about the vanity of idol worship and then at once went on to describe worship of the living God. A testimony like that from the town clerk of Ephesus speaks volumes; it helps us to get to know the preaching of Paul as dignified, positive, edifying, and not maligning or belittling.

In his farewell speech at Miletus, Paul describes his preaching in Ephesus in the following words: "*I did not shrink from declaring to you anything that was profitable and teaching you in public and from house to house, testifying both to Jews and to Greeks of repentance toward God and of faith in our Lord Jesus Christ*" (Acts 20:20–21). Earlier we called attention to these words as a clear sign that in all of Paul's missionary preaching repentance had a central place. In this connection we can add still another word spoken by him when he defended himself before King Agrippa (Acts 26:20). There he pointed out that he had declared to both Jews and Gentiles "*that they should repent and turn to God, performing deeds in keeping with their repentance.*" Here Paul uses two Greek words, one for repentance and another for turning or conversion: "*metanoein* (from *metanoia*, a change of mind), and *epistrephein* (from *epistrophē*, a change of attitude). Here again, repentance takes center stage. There is no mention of faith, since the person being addressed, Agrippa, was foreign to the faith.

Finally, we need to look at the conversation Paul had with Governor Felix and his wife Drusilla. It is summarized in Acts 24:24–26. Paul is given an opportunity to preach the gospel in a private conversation with two people. He starts by talking about righteousness and self-control, but he ends with a reference to the coming Judgment. Evidently, the first part of his talk with these people aimed at capturing their attention by addressing their sinful lifestyle. A governorship in the provinces, unfortunately, provided all too many opportunities for arbitrary rulings and perverted justice. Felix in his career was never able to steer clear of these wrongs, as is adequately shown by his treatment of Paul.[45] Moreover, this couple lived in excessive luxury and regal extravagance, a measure of affluence that all too easily smothered their conscience. Paul does not discuss sin in general, he does not expound on the nature of sin, but, like John the Baptist before him, he is utterly concrete and specific. He addresses people directly in their twisted lives and lost condition. Without offering any excuses or allowing for extenuating circumstances, he confronts these two high-placed persons with the judgment seat of Christ. His intention must have been to proceed from there to show something of the finished work of the Mediator, but once again, as so often in his life, he was not able to complete his message to the end. Felix dismissed him with a few lame words to the effect that he had heard enough for now and would summon him again at a more convenient time. Once again it strikes us that the apostle wished to attach the preaching of Christ to the declaration of judgment. He wanted to guide his audience past the Day of Judgment, on to the Cross. His discourse is constructed differently than in Lystra and Athens—it is more intimate and personal—but the main line is the

---

[45] [Felix kept Paul a prisoner, writes Luke, in the hope of a bribe for his release (Acts 24:26).]

same. Through Christ the Judge of the world, he wants to take them to Christ the Saviour of the world.

Why does Paul preach in this way?

We cannot avoid the question why the apostle Paul in general framed his preaching to the pagans in the specific way that we have thus far been able to establish. It has become clear to us that as a rule he followed a certain pattern, pursuing a line of argument that leads to the Cross. This pattern he hardly ever abandoned. Of course, he worked out his discourse differently in accordance with the circumstances each time. We have seen that the Pauline pattern ran the huge risk that his speech would be cut off before he could even mention the name of Christ, and that it therefore failed more than once in its aim to bring the message of Christ. Nonetheless, as the years went by the apostle made only slight changes in the structure of his discourse. Now then, if this is so, what are the reasons why Paul framed his gospel message on the mission field in this way?

This question is so important because it has been shown in the practice of missions of our own time that one of the most powerful tools is simply telling the story of the life and work of Jesus and his passion and death. More powerful than the most eloquent discourse to grip the pagan's heart is the plain narrative about One who voluntarily gave himself over to death in order to save others. The gospel itself is the best missionary: it does its mysterious work without anyone being there to explain it. Now then, are we to conclude that Paul deliberately scorned this excellent tool? Today, when we ask Christians on the mission field how they came to the faith, the answer will almost always be that they were fascinated by hearing the story of what Jesus has said and done. Yet Paul adopted an entirely different approach; his evangelistic messages were framed otherwise.

As we mull this over, we should take into account that we must not infer too much from the very minimal data about Paul's preaching that are found in the Book of Acts. They do not warrant far-reaching conclusions. We do, however, have reason to assume that the speech on Mars Hill has been passed on by Luke as the model for a speech to a pagan audience, and that Paul would have preached in the same vein at other places as well. Even then, we have to be careful about our conclusions. A public discourse, especially one addressed to an educated audience, demands quite a different approach than a private conversation. Who can say how Paul talked about the gospel to small groups of people in his workshop in Corinth or a lecture hall in Ephesus? In one place the apostle recalls that much of his work was done "from house to house" and by "night or day" (Acts 20:20, 31). In those long nightly conversations, he no doubt brought other things to the fore than those we heard him say in his public addresses. In other words, from the data Luke offers we must not infer more than what they say, being aware that they provide only a brief look at the method of preaching in public.

A second circumstance that we should take into account is the fact that the apostle was an itinerant preacher. There is always an element of hurry in what he does and writes, as if he is daily burdened with the thought that the gospel must be preached to all peoples and that therefore not a single hour of his existence may be wasted. He may have stayed in a city like Athens only a few days or weeks. Naturally, this factor also influenced his style of preaching. You speak in a different way when you are going to settle permanently in a place—and what you then say is only an introduction to further communications—than when you have only an hour and want to tackle paganism in its powerful hold on people. The discourse on Mars Hill is one grandiose attempt to address a motley company and confront it within the space of one hour with the very core of the gospel, namely that in Christ alone there is salvation from the coming wrath. A speech like that enters no sidetracks, tells no stories, gives no illustrations, but is steered with a firm hand toward the point it wants to make.

A third factor to reckon with is the nature of the audience. The men of Athens were trained in philosophy and wanted to test the philosophical merit of the teaching of this "babbler" (Acts 17:18). Granted, that was typically Athenian; yet the same inclination was found throughout the Greek world. Paul was fully justified when he said of the Greeks of his day: "*they seek wisdom*" (1 Cor. 1:22). The apostle always realized that he was not to give in to this specific hunger by way of relying on fancy rhetoric filled with "*wisdom of eloquent words*" and "*lofty speech*" (1 Cor. 1:17; 2:11). What he did do was to take up the questions that lived in the hearts of his hearers, framing his speech in such a way that something of the unfathomable wisdom of God would shine through his words. In the lecture halls on Mars Hill, amid the learned teachers of the day, Paul of Tarsus proclaimed the gospel of Christ with all the vital force that he by the grace of God possessed. There he stands as Raphael saw him: a man deeply moved with compassion and filled with a holy desire to display in that temple of human wisdom the splendor of God's good tidings. Ever so much had been thought about and pondered in Athens about the mysteries of the universe and about the Deity and his relation to humankind. Here Paul feels compelled to pit "*the folly of what we preach*" (1 Cor. 1:21) against the loftiest expressions of humanity's search for truth, and then the full light must fall on Him "*in whom are hidden all the treasures of wisdom and knowledge*" (Col. 2:3).

Finally, returning one more time to the pattern that Paul liked to use in his missionary preaching, we can only conclude that this pattern indeed enabled him to put into words, in a timely and relevant way, the core content of the gospel.

Paul invariably starts his discourse by speaking about God. That is only natural as well as necessary. The pagans too have thought about God; they have worshipped gods and lived life in their presence. Thus, for them God is not an unknown entity; on the contrary, they have well-defined notions about him. That is why Paul starts by talking about God and in a few broad strokes sketches the difference between the vanity of idol worship and the worship of the "living God." This living God is different from Zeus and Hermes, from Jupiter and Mercury. He also differs from the God of the philosophers, from the "Supreme Being," the "Universal Logos." By this strong preaching of the living God, Paul at the same time makes an appeal to what is revealed to them about God. After all, the pagans too have lived within range of God's revelation in his works, the revelation that goes out to all people, as the apostle explains at length in the first chapter of the Letter to the Romans. To be sure, they suppressed the truth in unrighteousness, but that suppressed truth continues to accuse them in their conscience. Pagans have a vague awareness that they are playing a game with the Almighty. With a resounding clarion call Paul awakens them from their addiction to that fatal game.

When Paul then draws a sharp line between, on the one hand "past generations" (Acts 14:16) and the "times of ignorance" (Acts 17:30), and on the other the time of the present, the new era, he indicates the mainspring, clear to all, behind his preaching. He is alluding to a widespread sense at the time, as mentioned earlier, that a new period of world history had begun. Very well, the hallmark of the new period of history is God's call to all nations to repent, a call of which Paul is but an obedient messenger. This whole exposition gives Paul's message a most lively and timely emphasis. It is a message directly related to the now, anchored in the history of the world.

Next, the demand for repentance is strongly reinforced by the announcement of judgment. The new era is also the last era. It is the historical period immediately preceding the Last Judgment. The Greek world of those days had a somewhat playful character; even its religions and its philosophies had something of a magic game, a game that was never fully serious because at every instant people kept a certain distance.[46] They thought about the deepest questions of life; they erected ethical systems, but they remained blithely on the sidelines; they worshiped their gods in magnificent temples, but inwardly they remained aloof. Contemporary culture displayed a frivolous feature of unreality. This lighthearted trait of the time is rudely interrupted by the terrifying news of a coming judgment. Greece first had to learn to tremble before the awesome seriousness of life itself and the coming Judgment, before it could see and behold the Son of Man. It would be useless to start off with preaching grace: you don't offer medicines to people who don't feel sick. Just as little as Christ, in response to the rich young ruler's question about what to do to inherit eternal life, could point him to the grace of God as the only way, so little could the apostle of the Gentiles start on Mars Hill by presenting the Cross as the salvation of the world. There has to be some awareness of guilt, some anxiety about being lost, if there is to be any search for the Saviour. Only when there is the sanction of judgment will people pay enough attention to the command to repent.

But then, amid the preaching of judgment there looms up the figure of Jesus Christ. In the Greek world, Christ is not first presented as the Man of Sorrows, as the great High Priest, but as the One authorized by God on Judgment Day. He is depicted as the man who rose from the dead and the appointed agent of the Creator of heaven and earth to deliver judgment in His name. Mankind shall be judged by the Man. The reason why Paul framed his preaching of the Christ in this fashion cannot be analyzed in any further detail because we know too little about what was going on in people's minds in those days. It is perfectly clear that it was impossible to plunge in with a message about a Cross, simply because the Cross cannot be preached until people feel the need for

---

[46] J. Huizinga, *Homo Ludens* (Haarlem: Tjeenk Willink, 1938), pp. 212ff [Eng. trans., *Homo Ludens: A Study of the Play-Element in Culture* (Boston: Beacon Press, 1955), pp. 146–152].

reconciliation and atonement. In the Jewish world, by contrast, people had participated in sacrificial ceremonies for centuries, and a gradual rise in prophecy had prepared them sufficiently for grasping what the Lamb of God would have to accomplish. In that context it was possible to begin with the Cross. The Greek world had also known its sacrifices; it too had its altars. But the omnipresence of these altars was no occasion to start preaching Him who was both altar and sacrifice. There must have been wise reasons to prompt the apostle of the Gentiles not to mention the name of Jesus until he had mentioned the coming judgment.

Once that was mentioned, the road was clear to depict the same Jesus as the *Sōtēr*, the Saviour who can deliver us from the coming wrath. We can no longer ascertain how the apostle would have elaborated this last bit of his speech, but we do know that his whole address was intended to issue in this last part and find its conclusion there.

Christ himself once prophesied that the Comforter, the Holy Spirit of God, would "*convict the world of sin and righteousness and judgment*" (John 16:8). It must be said of the Greek world that on its own, despite its many profound systems of philosophy, it had learned nothing of "sin and righteousness and judgment." It held that man was chained to matter, that the body was the prison of the soul, that evil passions were like untamed horses that conducted human life along yawning ravines. It spoke of world-flight and the ascetic life as the only way to be freed from seductive lusts. But it did not know *sin*, did not recognize sin for what it is. It spoke about this world as a harmonious whole, as suffused with divine reason, the Logos; it was keenly alive to the marvelous connections in the structure of the cosmos. But it did not understand the law of *righteousness*. It dreamed on, living for games and gymnastics, for amateur discussions and debates, for worship in marble temples under azure skies, for festive processions and all-night revelry. But it had not an inkling of the coming *judgment*. In the marketplaces of Asia Minor and Greece, Paul, driven by the Holy Spirit, convicted the world of sin and righteousness and judgment, in order that from the penitential preaching of the Judgment might be born the opportunity to display something of the mystery of grace through the Cross of Christ our Lord.

5. The Mystery of Mars Hill

[22] Men of Athens, I perceive that in every way you are very religious.
[23] For as I passed along and observed the objects of your worship, I found also
an altar with this inscription, TO THE UNKNOWN GOD. What therefore you
worship as unknown, this I proclaim to you.
[24] The God who made the world and everything in it, being Lord of heaven
and earth, does not live in temples made by man,
[25] nor is he served by human hands, as though he needed anything, since he
himself gives to all mankind life and breath and everything.
[26] And he made from one man every nation of mankind, to live on all the face
of the earth, having determined allotted periods and the boundaries of their
dwelling place,
[27] that they should seek God, in the hope that they might feel their way toward him and find him. Yet he is actually nor far from each one of us,
[28] for "In him we live and move and have our being," as some of your own
poets have said. "For we are indeed his offspring."
[29] Being then God's offspring, we ought not to think that the divine being is
like gold or silver or stone, an image formed by the art and imagination of man.
[30] The times of ignorance God overlooked, but now he commands all people
everywhere to repent,
[31] because he has fixed a day on which he will judge the world in righteousness
by a man whom he has appointed; and of this he has given assurance to all by
raising him from the dead.

Multiple opinions

A great variety of interpretations exists of Paul's speech on Mars Hill as recorded in Acts chapter 17.[47] Our previous chapter has already discussed this

---

[47] [The variety of interpretations is reflected in the choice made by English translators of the Greek word *deisidaimonesterous* in Paul's opening statement. Most versions have him describe the Athenians as "very religious in every way," but the old KJV has Paul calling them straight out "too superstitious," while other translations paraphrase

speech at some length, but there is one question that we have thus far carefully avoided, and that is what might be called the *gentleness* of this speech. And in that connection we face a second question, namely about the *respect* shown by Paul for pagan philosophy.

The speech on Mars Hill is gentle, moderate, if not lenient. That strikes us already at a first superficial reading. In the beginning of the speech Paul commends the Athenians for being "*very religious in every way.*" Next, he mentions the altar erected "to the unknown god" and follows it up by starting to talk about the Creator of heaven and earth (vs. 24). In verse 29 he briefly touches on the sin of idol worship, but he does so in the mildest of words: "*We ought not to think that the divine being is like gold or silver or stone.*" "We ought not to think!" The Old Testament prophets certainly tended to use rather more robust language when they fulminated against idol worship. How Isaiah could mock those who bowed before images of wood or stone! Paul expresses himself courteously, amicably, carefully.

In verse 30 he says that God overlooked "the times of ignorance"—again very mild words. All those centuries of pagan apostasy and idolatry are smoothed over as "times of ignorance." And he adds that God does not want to remember them anymore and now commands all people everywhere to turn to Him. Not a word about sin! The pagans of Mars Hill are very religious and have always known that they were God's offspring, only they were living in ignorance. They are blind souls who need to have their eyes opened and who need a change of mind. No mention of the sin of living in alienation from God, an abomination that the ancient prophets so fulminated against.

Closely connected with this gentleness are the references to what pagan poets and philosophers have said. After quoting with approval a line from one of those poets, Paul continues by alluding to ideas found among pagan philosophers. Particularly the Stoics are referenced with approval for having said remarkably true things.

What are we to make of this? Does Paul mean to praise Stoicism as a kind of prototype of the gospel? Does he view those philosophical writings as an ally against crude and shallow paganism? Does he regard pagan writings too as inspired by God's Spirit? — But doesn't he realize that those Stoic philosophers

---

still more freely: "overmuch given to fear of the gods" (Basic English), or more literally: "given up to demon worship" (Darby).]

meant something altogether different from what he reads in their words? Has it escaped his attention that this old philosophy is out and out unchristian and unspiritual? In short, why does Paul use such extraordinarily sympathetic words about what pagan authors have said? How could he do this?

Such is the mystery of Mars Hill. It is a mystery that seems to defy all explanation. Small wonder that over the centuries all kinds of opinions have been put forward about the questions it raises.

In the first period of the Christian church, various theologians tended to ascribe great value to the products of Greek philosophy. They saw philosophy as a powerful aid in spreading the gospel. For example, Justin Martyr (born circa 100 A.D.) put it this way:

> The teachings of Plato are not completely different from those of Christ, but they are not the same in all respects, nor are the teachings of others, such as Stoics and poets and historians. For each man spoke well in proportion to the share he had of the Logos.... Whatever has rightly been said among men is the property of us Christians.... For all the writers were able to see reality darkly thanks to the seed of the Logos in them.[48]

And in another place the same Justin Martyr expressed himself as follows:

> We have taught that Christ, as the Logos of whom all men are partakers, is the first-born of God, and those who have lived according to the Logos are Christians, even though they have been called atheists, such as Greeks like Socrates and Heraclitus, and men like them.[49]

Clement of Alexandria (born 150 A.D.) spoke in the same vein. In his major work *The Stromata*, in a passage dealing with philosophy, he makes the following remark:

[48] Justin Martyr, *Apologia*, 2.13.
[49] *Apologia*, 1.46.

> ... before the coming of Christ, the Greeks needed philosophy for righteousness, but now philosophy has become conducive to piety, since it is a kind of preparatory training to those who attain to the faith through demonstration.... For philosophy was a *paidagōgos* [tutor] to bring the Greeks to Christ, as the law did the Hebrews.[50]

Clement uses the same word *paidagōgos* that Paul uses in Galatians 3:24, where he calls the law a "schoolmaster" to bring us to Christ.

These utterances could easily be multiplied with many others. They all show that in the Early Church it was believed that the Greek philosophers, in particular Socrates, Plato, and the Stoics, were not far from the kingdom of God. Presumably, led by the Spirit of God, they saw from afar, as it were, something of the truth that was to be revealed in the gospel. To be sure, these ancient theologians did assume that Plato and the other philosophers of Greece borrowed many ideas from the prophets of the Old Testament. Clement does not even hesitate to call them "thieves and robbers" because prior to the coming of Christ they "stole" multiple parts of the truth from the Hebrew prophets.[51] Yet all this shows that they did see a gulf between the gospel and pagan idolatry but not between the gospel and the teachings of the philosophers. We who live so many centuries later can see in hindsight that the Early Church paid a big price for this congenial stance towards philosophy. She recognized too little the godless character of this philosophy and as a result was often seduced too readily to all kinds of error. But then the question arises, had Paul in his Mars Hill speech not given encouragement to this congenial attitude? Did Paul himself not go much too far in his appreciation of what pagan poets and philosophers had said? And is all that sympathy shown for the writings of the philosophers in the centuries that followed not the inevitable consequence of the speech pattern followed by the great apostle?

Later missiological studies have had a lot to say about Paul's speech in Athens. Catholic authors were happy to refer to it as evidence that Paul did not regard all of pagan religion as a work of the devil: after all, he quotes pagan writers and his whole speech bears a Stoic character to make it attractive for a purely Greek

[50] Clement of Alexandria, *Stromata*, 1.5.
[51] Ibid., 1.17.

audience.[52] And the great Protestant missiologist Gustav Warneck considers the speech "a typical example of a point of contact for missions,"[53] and his son Johannes Warneck commends it as "an unsurpassed example of preaching to the pagans."[54]

Missionaries who saw themselves compelled to wrestle personally with the problem of how to preach on the mission field, could not help but see in the apostle's speech a brilliant example of a prudent approach, even though they sometimes worried whether a method like that—taking as a point of contact what pagans had come up with—might not entail dangerous consequences. Anyone who today were to venture and proclaim the gospel in India or China or Japan with the use of citations from what these peoples themselves have experienced and expressed would as a rule find out soon enough that to preach like that has the big advantage that he can captivate his audience, but at the same time that it has the significant drawback that he cannot be sufficiently clear about the sharp dividing line between the gospel and pagan philosophy.

A literary approach

In recent years the study of the Areopagus address has entered a new stage. A literary approach to the text has been introduced in the scholarly world. This approach was launched by a sensational publication by the great classical philologist Eduard Norden (1868–1941), which appeared in 1913 under the title *Agnostos Theos.*[55] Norden's book carefully examined the entire speech on Mars Hill, in particular as to its form, and tested it against what we know about other, similar speeches.

With respect to the form and style of the speech, Norden is of the opinion that it strongly resembles what other religious preachers of the day were accustomed to saying. A certain Philostratus wrote a biography of a religious teacher

---

[52] J. Thauren, *Die Akkommodation im katholischen Heidenapostolat* (Münster: Aschendorff, 1927), p. 12.

[53] G. Warneck, *Evangelische Missionslehre,* 3 vols. (Gotha: Perthes, 1897–1900), III/2: 95.

[54] J. Warneck, *Paulus im Lichte der heutigen Heidenmission* (Berlin: Rothers, 1914), p. 73.

[55] Eduard Norden, *Agnostos Theos. Untersuchungen zur Formengeschichte religiöser Rede* (Leipzig and Berlin: Teubner, 1923) [7th impr. 1996; the title translates as "The Unknown God: Investigations Concerning the History of Religious Speech"].

of the time named Apollonius of Tyana. It contains information about the many disputations that Apollonius conducted in Athens with adherents of the Eleusinian mysteries. It also relates a saying of the same Apollonius that it is advisable to speak about all the gods with respect, "especially in Athens, where altars to unknown gods have also been erected." Putting two and two together, Norden concludes that the Apollonius in question once held a religious discourse in which he took as his point of departure the same altar inscription that is mentioned in Acts. If one keeps in mind that Apollonius first had disputations, followed by a discourse in which he alluded to the same inscription, then according to Norden it is perfectly clear that the redactor of Paul's Areopagus speech was familiar with the story of Apollonius and constructed his account on the basis of the data available to him about the works of Apollonius. In that case it is not possible that Paul himself gave that speech. The whole story about the speech was composed by someone else in light of the story of Apollonius.

As his study proceeds, Norden highlights that the Areopagus speech is brimming with philosophical ideas and expressions. That commences at once with the expression "the unknown god." Norden points out that we do not know whether altars were ever erected to an "unknown god" anywhere else in Antiquity, but we do know that in that age there were altars dedicated to "unknown gods" (plural). Thus, the author of the Areopagus speech changed the plural to the singular. Norden ascribes this change to gnostic and Neoplatonist influences, while all manner of Eastern notions were at work as well.

All sorts of other words and expressions in Paul's speech betray, writes Norden, Hellenistic and especially Stoic influence. For instance, the word "feel" in verse 27—that all the nations of the world should seek God "*in the hope that they might feel their way toward him and find him*"—is typically Stoic. And the expression "*not far from each one of us*" is likewise based on Stoic notions. Again, the argument that God is not served "*as though he needed anything*" is found in a variety of forms in Stoic writings. In sum, on the basis of his research Norden arrives at the conclusion that the philosophical portion of this speech is composed of all kinds of loose threads "extracted from the fabric of Stoic philosophy."[56] A kind of theological jargon had developed in those days under the influence of Stoicism. Already in the last centuries before Christ, this jargon

---

[56] E. Norden, *Agnostos Theos*, p. 29.

was touched up with a bit of Semitic veneer and therefore lent itself exceedingly well later for Christian evangelism. The speech on Mars Hill, as framed by a Christian redactor, was happy to employ in its own fashion this language of Stoic theologians, and in so doing laid the groundwork for the development of Christian thought in the centuries to follow. That is the "world-historical significance" of the discourse as recorded in Acts 17.[57]

Norden's carefully constructed and amply documented book has long had a profound influence on opinions about the Areopagus speech. Johannes Weiss, who wrote a work on the Early Church, says about it that one cannot even begin to understand the speech if one does not have recourse to Greek philosophy. When Paul says that "*in him we live and move and have our being*," it not only sounds like Stoic pantheism: it *is* pantheism. The whole of Paul's speech rests on the idea that the new *Offenbarungs-religion* (revealed religion) is nothing other than humanity's universal rational religion, and that is why it can accommodate all philosophical ideas.[58] Many others have drawn the same conclusion, both philologists and theologians.

This view was reinforced when it became more and more likely that the expression "*in him we live and move and have our being*" was likewise of Greek origin. The following observation about the expression was made in a Syrian commentary on the Acts of the Apostles, written by Isho'dad of Merv, bishop in Hadatha (9th century A.D.) and translated and published in Britain in 1913:

> With respect to these words it should be noted that because the Cretans proclaimed as truth about Zeus "that he was a tyrant, that he was torn apart by a wild boar and buried, and behold, his grave is known among us," therefore Minos, the son of Zeus, delivered a eulogy about his father in which he said, "A grave was made for Thee, O holy and exalted One, by the lying Cretans, those evil beasts and lazy bellies, for Thou art never dead: Thou art alive and remaineth

[57] Ibid, p. 127.
[58] Joh. Weiss, *Das Urchristentum*, pp. 180–181.

alive, for in Thee we live and move and have our being." Thus it was from Minos that St Paul quoted those words.[59]

Granted, a great deal is still uncertain about this observation, yet it does not appear improbable that indeed these words of Paul are based on a Greek poem. The word of Isho'dad even gains in weight when we recall that Paul was familiar with the above judgment of the Cretans (see Titus 1:12). Zeus is called the living one, who does not die, in whom we all have life. Word derivation in the Greek of the time tended to connect the word Zeus to the verb *zēn*, which means "to live." Thus, his very name indicates that he cannot be dead. In the Mars Hill speech Paul supposedly took a word that was originally intended to say something about Zeus and applied it to God himself.[60] And the citation that followed, taken from a poem by Aratus entitled "Phaenomena," was also originally intended to teach something about Zeus: "For we are indeed his offspring."[61]

A few years ago these things again came in for attention through an interesting study by Professor Dibelius of Heidelberg about "Paul on the Areopagus."[62] Dibelius, too, sees all kinds of Stoic expressions loom before his eyes. For example, that people "seek God" may seem to be, in and of itself, an Old Testament concept, because also in the Old Testament mention is often made of people "seeking" God. However, cautions Dibelius, that seeking is something entirely

---

[59] *The Commentaries of Isho'dad of Merv, Bishop of Hadatha in Syriac and English*. Vol. 4, *Acts of the Apostles*, ed. and trans. by Margaret Dunlop Gibson (Cambridge UP, 1913). Cf. R. H. Woltjer, "De jongste onderzoekingen over de rede op den Areopagus en de christelijke beschouwingen der Oudheid." In *Wetenschappelijke samenkomst van de Vrije Universiteit* (Amsterdam: Kirchner, 1917), pp. 55ff.

[60] Cf. Kirsopp Lake, et al., *The Beginnings of Christianity*, IV, 215, 216. [The "Hymn to Zeus," written by the poet Cleanthes (330–230 B.C.), a leading spokesman of Stoicism, contains the following lines: "Hail to Thee, O Zeus! It is right for us to call upon Thee, since from Thee we have our being, . . . whose lot it is to be God's image, we alone of all mortal creatures that live upon the earth."]

[61] Kirsopp Lake, et al. *The Beginnings of Christianity*, IV, 218. [The poem "Phaenomena" by Aratus (310–240 B.C.) opens with the following lines: "Let us begin with Zeus, whom we mortals never leave unspoken. / For every street, every marketplace is full of Zeus. / Even the sea and the harbor are full of this deity. / Everyone everywhere is indebted to Zeus. / For we are indeed his offspring."]

[62] M. Dibelius, *Paulus auf dem Areopagus* (Heidelberg: Winter Verlag, 1939) [see also M. Dibelius, "Paul on the Areopagus," in his *Studies in the Acts of the Apostles* (London, 1956)].

different from what is meant here. In the former case it is a matter of the will, whereas here is meant an act of the mind, of rational thought. "Seeking God" in the Areopagus speech is not Old Testament language; clearly, it is Greek language.[63] Further, Dibelius also accentuates the gentle character of the speech. The former days are called "the times of ignorance," which God "overlooks," i.e., which He "looks past." The least possible guilt is ascribed to the pagans themselves; their entire idolatry is virtually excused as lack of knowledge and interpreted as attempts to seek God.[64] "What we have in front of us, therefore," writes Dibelius, "is a Hellenistic discourse on the true knowledge of God." The last sentence from that speech, the sentence in which Paul speaks of the coming of the Risen One to judge the world, "is the only Christian sentence in the whole Areopagus speech." What is more, all kinds of ideas that are expressed in the speech are diametrically opposed to what Paul argued emphatically in his epistles, so that it is absolutely impossible to view the speech on the Areopagus as an address delivered by Paul himself. The author of the Book of Acts must have invented it and put the words into Paul's mouth. Paul himself would never have talked in such extenuating terms about paganism. On the contrary, he makes clear in Romans chapter 1 that paganism is a flight from God, a denial of God, an exchange of God's glory for unworthy human inventions. That is how the real Paul argues; he brings out that no one seeks God, "*no, not one*" (Rom. 3:11). The Areopagus speech carefully and kindly flatters paganism. It' is as if Paul understands nothing of what separates the gospel of Christ from even the most noble expressions of pagan thinkers. Thus, there is a deep gulf between the real Paul of the epistles and the fictitious Paul of the sermon in Acts 17.[65]

The world-famous missionary Albert Schweitzer has also written about Paul's speech on the Areopagus, and his opinion is also dismissive. He views the words "in him we live and move and have our being" as an arresting expression of Stoic pantheistic mysticism, which sees God as the force that pervades all of nature and also dwells in man—a pagan idea, not Christian. Paul himself taught

---

[63] Dibelius, *Paulus auf dem Areopagus*, p. 9.

[64] Ibid., p. 34.

[65] Ibid., pp. 34–43. See also Gerhard Kittel and Gerhard Friedrich, *Theologisches Wörterbuch zum Neuen Testament* (Stuttgart: Verlag von W. Kohlhammer, 1932 and following) [English: Geoffrey W. Bromiley et al., *Theological Dictionary of the New Testment* (Grand Rapids: Wm. B. Eerdmans, 1964 and following)], III, 718, s.v. *kineo*.

a wholly different mysticism in his epistles, namely the "Christ mysticism," whereby we indeed become one with Christ, and through Christ will one day also become one with God. But this Christ mysticism of Paul is altogether different from the mysticism of the speech on the Areopagus. Accordingly, Schweitzer too leans toward the view that the speech was never held by Paul but made up by the author of Acts.[66]

Paul's speech in more recent theology

To be complete, we should point out that more recently a remarkable shift has occurred in the assessment of the speech on the Areopagus and the questions associated with it. We owe this shift especially to the Swiss theologian Karl Barth. Barth as well as his pupils have occupied themselves explicitly with the whole question of the message of Christ and its relation to the other religions. Naturally, this discussion has often involved the Mars Hill speech and has resulted in an entirely different conclusion about it than had become customary.

Take, for example, the view of Johannes Witte in his book about the gospel and world religions.[67] In this book Witte deals extensively with the speech of Paul found in Acts 17, but he views it quite differently than Norden and Dibelius and many others. He emphasizes that the speech is a call to repentance and that the idea that we are God's offspring should be understood in that light. We are no longer God's offspring in the true sense of the word, for everything in us is broken by sin. That Paul mentions that God is not far from us—indeed, that we live and move and have our being in Him—is in no sense meant as an excuse. On the contrary, it indicates instead that the ignorance which is exhibited so dramatically in the altar to the "unknown God" is *culpable* ignorance. God is not far from man, yet man erects altars to unknown gods because he does not hear God's voice, because he has abandoned God, because God's call no longer gets through to him. Today, however, God is willing, if these pagans believe Him and accept his grace, to ignore former times of ignorance. He is willing to forgive

---

[66] Albert Schweitzer, *Die Mystik des Apostels Paulus* (Tübingen: Mohr, 1930), pp. 6–10 [Eng. trans., *The Mysticism of Paul the Apostle,* 2nd ed. (London: Black, 1953), pp. 6–9].

[67] Johannes Witte, *Die Christusbotschaft und die Religionen* (Göttingen: Vandenhoeck & Ruprecht, 1936).

the Greeks for their "entire, glorious history with their pagan religions and their philosophy, with their thinkers and their poets."[68]

The call to repentance at the end of the speech clearly shows, according to Witte, that the reference to the inscription on the altar is not meant to be an acknowledgment that the Greeks too did know a little bit about God, but that it should be seen much more as a serious indictment that they thought of the Creator of heaven and earth as *agnostos*, as "unknown." Accordingly, this speech ought to be read as a call to turn away from this darkness, including philosophic darkness, and to turn instead toward the light—to turn from the power of Satan to the true God. The Paul of Mars Hill is the same Paul that we meet in the Epistles. He may be saying things differently, but when we read his words more closely we discover that Mars Hill condemns paganism and pagan philosophy as much as do the Epistles.

Why so gentle?

Now that we have briefly canvassed the various views that have been offered about the speech on Mars Hill, its mystery stands before us in all its puzzling nature. We do well to take it apart for a moment and examine each component on its own. The first question we must then address is the apparent gentleness so characteristic of the speech.

Where does this gentle character appear most noticeably? First off, we could point to the salutation in which the apostle calls the Athenians people "*who in every way are very religious*." The Greek word Paul uses here stems from the word *deisidaimōn*, which is a very neutral word that can be used in both a good and a bad sense. Thus, it need not have been meant as praise in the mouth of the apostle.[69] The hearers of course may have heard it as praise, but that says nothing about what Paul meant.

Furthermore, it can be considered gentle and moderate that nowhere in the speech is the word sin mentioned. In Lystra the apostle in hot indignation had talked of the "vain things" that people were guilty of, but in Athens he issues no

[68] Witte, *Die Christusbotschaft und die Religionen*, pp. 41ff.

[69] Kirsopp Lake says that the word means "religiosity" more than it signifies "religion," and he adds: "it is certainly not intended to be complimentary." *The Beginnings of Christianity*, IV, 274. See also Kittel, *Theologisches Wörterbuch zum Neuen Testament*, s.v. *deisidaimōn*.

such condemnation. It is all only "ignorance," an ignorance that seems all the more excusable because it is coupled with piety. Those men of Athens: poor fellows, erecting altars to "the unknown god," seeking God in the hope of finding him, yet without success. Wouldn't you almost start blaming God for not having spoken more clearly to these religious folk?

As we pose these questions we must be on guard against misleading interpretations and incorrect assessments. In the first place, we need to remind ourselves that we are looking here at a missionary sermon. One can try to convince people of sin in many different ways. There are situations in which one does best by addressing the audience as a "brood of vipers" and telling them flat-out in what ways they are sinning. In a sermon on the mission field, however, gentler methods are generally more effective and more even-handed. It is still our daily experience in missions that a soft hint, a mild prompt is far more effective than a blunt word. The people of the Far East are exceedingly sensitive on this score: a hard word can often embarrass and embitter them, while a very subtle allusion is often able to convince them of the wrong they have done. Sometimes just one question, "Wouldn't it have been better if you had . . ." has proved to be a more powerful way to preach sin than a direct allegation. This is true about the mission field, and in general wherever we are dealing with people who are as yet ignorant of the gospel.[70]

Accordingly, we must read the Mars Hill speech in such a way that we are not misled by all those sympathetic words. And then it is at once obvious that the entire speech must be read in terms of the word *repentance* which occurs at the end of verse 30. If it is true that the Athenians must repent, then their ignorance evidently is culpable ignorance; then it is sin. That need not be stated baldly; the sages of Athens undoubtedly got the hint. That word *repentance* imparts to all the other words a very specific content; it colors them in a very special way. The men of Athens may initially have thought that Paul wanted to excuse their ignorance, but gradually their eyes will have been opened to the fact that this preacher from Tarsus approached the big questions of religion and thought in a totally different manner than their own philosophers. He spoke of *metanoia*, repentance, even of a coming judgment. Mentioning those two things transformed all those other things, however mildly and moderately stated, into

---

[70] It goes without saying, of course, that within the orbit of a church, among people who know better, one must act more directly and forcefully.

a serious indictment. Harnack already pointed out that the "ignorance" mentioned in this speech is characterized, implicitly yet clearly enough, as guilt.[71]

But then what is the meaning of the statement that God was willing to "overlook" or "look past" the times of ignorance? Doesn't that mean that God does not think it is all that bad, that He considers the sin of ignorance excusable? The word "overlook" must be read, however, in the light of what follows. God overlooked the former times of ignorance, but "*now He commands all people everywhere to repent*." These last words make it clear as daylight that *to overlook* certainly does not include *to forgive sin*. If that were the case, repentance would no longer be necessary, for then the former sin would no longer be counted. Paul wants to depict the proclamation of repentance as a token of God's unmerited favour. There were plenty of reasons to let the nations wander about in their culpable ignorance, but now this inscrutable fact presents itself that despite that ignorance, God, while overlooking the times of ignorance, in his infinite compassion comes down to man and calls him to repent, lest he be lost. The proclamation of repentance is therefore a token of gracious kindness, of "overlooking." It is an act of grace, even though grace in the deepest sense of the word does not become the portion of man until it leads him to repentance. In other words, "to overlook" does not mean "to turn a blind eye to," as if the ignorance didn't matter; it is no weakening of the culpable nature of ignorance. On the contrary, it presupposes its culpable nature. Paul wants to move his audience on Mars Hill into viewing his address as an amazing token of divine concern with man, one that ought to amaze us all the more because man was trapped in sinful ignorance.

Gospel and philosophy

There remains the question that is much more difficult: Why does Paul quote all kinds of words from pagan philosophies with so much approval? A lot can be said against the philosophical arguments of Eduard Norden—in particular the parallel he draws between an episode in the life of Apollonius and Paul's performance on Mars Hill, and the conclusion he then arrives at[72]—but one

---

[71] Adolph Harnack, *Mission und Ausbreitung des Christentums*, I, 392 [Eng. trans. I, 476 n. 2e].

[72] On this, cf. R. H. Woltjer, "De jongste onderzoekingen over de rede op den Areopagus en de Christelijke beschouwingen der Oudheid," pp. 64ff.

thing we must grant Norden: the apostle makes ample use of words and phrases that were said by pagan authors. Are we allowed to infer from this that the apostle affirms those sayings of pagan authors, that he regards them as divine revelation cloaked in Greek philosophy? As we have seen, the old Apologetic Fathers indeed often considered various words from Greek philosophers as a kind of *praeparatio evangelica* and took those words to be divine revelation. Even Augustine still held the view that in the thoughts of Plato and others only a "change of a few words and sentiments"[73] would be needed to bring them into conformity with the gospel. Clement of Alexandria, who likewise attached great value to Greek philosophy, appeals explicitly to Paul's speech on the Areopagus: "This shows that he [Paul], by availing himself even of poetical examples from the 'Phenomena' of Aratus, approved of what had been well said by the Greeks."[74] In other words, Clement is of the opinion that the Areopagus speech indeed places the seal of approval on the finest utterances of Greek thought.

Again, it will be necessary to weigh carefully if we are not to be seduced into making big mistakes. And then it is imperative that we draw attention to the fact that we are dealing here with a speech made on the mission field. When Paul subsequently talks about paganism, in Romans chapter 1, he can say all sorts of things in a different and sharper voice than when he faced a group of pagans in person. One must really have stood once before such an audience and have personally agonized over what to say to a throng of people to whom every expression in the gospel is foreign—to say them so that they can understand what they mean. There are experienced missionaries who have often addressed a non-Christian audience and who have the feeling each time that it is an unimaginably heavy task. Many of them feel somewhat inhibited when fellow-Christians are present in the audience, a feeling that does not stem from cowardice but solely from fear that these fellow-Christians will apply the wrong criteria. Why does Paul not speak in Athens about the Cross? Why does he not even mention the name of Jesus? I repeat, people would have judged the speech on Mars Hill differently if they had studied it, not in their study, but on the mission field. Men like Norden and Dibelius and many others never understood it. They adduced all kinds of parallels from contemporary Hellenistic literature and put their finger on contrasts between the Paul of the Areopagus and the

[73] "paucis mutatis verbis atque sententiis." Augustine, *De vera religione*, 4.7.

[74] Clement, *Stromata*, 1.19.

Paul of the Epistles, but they never realized that an evangelistic sermon demands an altogether different approach from the preacher than a presentation of fundamental principles in a circle of kindred spirits. It would not have been difficult for Paul to speak the same way in Athens as he had done in Antioch of Pisidia (Acts 13:16–42). Then he would not have used a single Stoic expression but have stayed within the framework of the Old Testament. But then his Athenian audience would not have fallen prey to any misunderstandings, for the simple reason that they would not have understood one syllable of what he was saying. The foremost criterion a missionary is obliged to follow is that his message should arrest the attention of his hearers and speak to their hearts in the language they are used to.

Keeping this in mind, is it any wonder that Paul weaves all kinds of expressions in his message that were familiar to the intellectuals of his day? In his book about *Paul the Apostle* A. M. Brouwer correctly points out that missions always encounters the same difficulty that Paul faced on Mars Hill. When in the 19th century Dr. Neubronner van der Tuuk went to North Sumatra to work among the Batak people and translate the Bible into their language, he was forced to use many words which up until that time all had a pagan content.[75] Since then, Christian churches have grown and spread in the region and when their members now read that early translation it makes a pagan impression on them.[76] When a text like John 1:1, to use another example, is translated into Chinese with the words "*In the beginning was the Tao*," then this translation, to be sure, integrates the text into Chinese thought as a whole, yet it is clear that any Chinese person that reads it can easily come to misunderstand it. All rendering of the gospel into another language forces translators to reach for terminology that is indigenous among that particular people, even though every one of the words they employ is loaded with former, unchristian ideas.

Now then, there was all the more reason for Paul to use expressions of the philosophy of his day, because that philosophy was indeed used by God as a preparation for what was to come. The Greek world, speaking through its poets and intellectuals, had come to the conclusion that the old polytheism was folly

---

[75] [The Batak people were a group of tribes that practiced cannibalism. During the 19th century, missions on the island of Sumatra in the Dutch East Indies was a race between Islam and Christianity in which the former made more converts than the latter.]

[76] A. M. Brouwer, *Paulus de Apostel*, II, 125–126.

and that this world instead was ruled by one omnipotent divine Being. It had also come to understand something of the wise ordinances by which God rules this world, and it had celebrated the wisdom of God in a variety of ways. It had done so in the wrong sense, for the god they worshiped was seen as an impersonal, divine force that inhabits all living things, that causes flowers to bloom and pervades man and animal, but that god was not seen as a Lord who reigns and commands. Greek philosophers got more and more entangled in a new kind of polytheism colored by mysticism; hence they lacked the strength to introduce reforms. They left the old temples alone and tolerated idol worship, at most mocking it, but they did not turn their backs on it in holy indignation. The piety and devotion of that Hellenistic world degenerated into artificiality and empty rhetoric because it was not borne up by genuine fear of God. Nonetheless, it is fair to say that the entire degenerative process of Greek paganism and the awakening of philosophical thought and the intellectual search for truth were the fruits of God's compassionate concern with a culture that had sunk very low. One can maintain this even if one is convinced that the Greek world in its thoughts and intentions had lost the way and that therefore all the beautiful things it had spoken must be called, in the sense in which they meant it, a lie. It is not without importance in this connection to point to the influence of the Greek translation of the Old Testament – the Septuagint – may be seen as yet another sign of God's care and concern, preparing the world for that which was to come.

If we take all this into consideration and then read Paul's address again, many problems do become simpler.

The apostle starts by mentioning the altar to the "unknown god" (vs. 23). We recall that Norden cites a passage in a biography of Apollonius which states that Athens, too, had "altars to unknown gods." However, a careful reading of this statement should convince us that it does not at all imply that every one of the altars in question was dedicated to "unknown gods" (plural); it can just as well mean that there were several altars, each of which would have been dedicated to an "unknown god."[77] Paul had seen an altar like that as he walked about Athens, and this inscription had greatly distressed him.

---

[77] See also my *Christus en de mystiek van het Oosten* (Kampen: Kok, 1934), pp. 120–128 [Eng. trans., "Christ and Asian Mysticism," in *The J. H. Bavinck Reader*, 301–411, at 317–323].

Now, we can leave aside what the sponsor of this altar meant by it. Most probably, he was particularly afflicted or particularly blessed and felt the need to call upon a special god but didn't know which. The Greek world had gods of the sea and gods of the rivers; it worshiped mountain gods and forest gods; it acknowledged deities that covered the whole range of human life. But conceivably there might be instances when people did not know to which god to turn. Thus this sponsor probably erected his altar to the "unknown god," to the god whose name he didn't know but whom he did want to petition or thank. If we read it this way, the altar is a symptom of the boundlessness of paganism. It knows countless gods, but it never has gods enough. New situations can arise at any time when no one knows to which god to turn. Paganism is like an avalanche: it is always expanding, it never finds its boundaries, and as a result new altars keep appearing, dedicated to unknown gods. It is easy to get lost in a plethora of gods and spirits. Paul stood still at that altar and it moved him deeply. As in a flash he saw the tragedy of paganism, that eternal seeking and groping, that perpetual inquiring and inventing, never coming to rest. And at that moment the altar for that one "unknown god" became for him an unmistakable hallmark of all pagan religions. Pagan religion erects altars for gods, invents stories about those gods, gives them names, but in the end it gets all tangled up; it tires of its fantasies, of making up fairy tales. Exhausted, it finally dedicates its worship to an "unknown god." An altar is built, sacrifices are offered, and pious prayers are raised without knowing whom to address or whom to fear and revere.

Standing on Mars Hill, the apostle calls that altar to mind. "You worship something of which you say yourself that you don't know what it is." Has Paul found an *Anknüpfungspunkt* in paganism, a "point of contact" with pagan thought that he finds useful? I am inclined to answer this question in the negative. Paul is not in any way "connecting" with some positive element in pagan religion or pagan philosophy. His point of departure is solely the admission of poverty and ignorance which pagan seekers have themselves acknowledged. If the apostle had begun by stating on his own authority that the Greeks did not know God, they would most likely have been offended and sent him away. But now he catches paganism in one of those honest moments in which it admits itself that it "knows not God," in which it acknowledges that its worship has no address because they utterly lack any clear knowledge of God. In other words, Paul treats that one inscription on an altar as a symptom of the whole of Greek religious worship. There were of course countless altars in Athens that did have an inscription dedicated to a specific god or goddess, but those too were at bottom dedicated to the great "Unknown," for all the names that were given to those gods were made up. Here, in the circle of Athenian poets and philosophers, the apostle can calmly say these things because for a long time already Greek philosophers had poured out their vials of critique upon the worship of divine beings, and the same philosophy had ended in acknowledging one divine being, a divine Reason, which mysteriously pervades the whole universe. Suddenly Paul draws himself up and says, "What you worship as unknown, this I proclaim." I stand here before you as one who knows, as one who can give you the Name of the nameless, who can remove the veil before which so many generations have trembled.

In the texts that follow (vss. 24 and 25), the apostle delivers in short sentences a sermon about God. He uses a few words to express grand and majestic things. He proclaims God as the "Maker of heaven and earth," as the perfect Spirit who "does not dwell in temples made by man," as the Blessed One who "does not need" our poor and paltry worship. These words can be seen as the turning point of the whole speech. Paul may be using words in places that were also used by Stoic thinkers whenever they talked about the World Reason or the World Soul, but, coming from Paul's mouth, these words acquire a new sound, because he is not talking about some Thing, a Force, a Being, but about some One, about a God who stands before us as a Person, as a Lord. In vs. 23 Paul is still speaking in neutral terms, saying that "what you worship, this I proclaim." But then it turns personal: it is no longer a What but a Who, a personal God, a God who lays His hands on us as His creatures. Thereby all those many expressions used by Paul are raised to an infinitely higher level than pagan seekers and thinkers had ever reached. Here Stoicism stops; here Neoplatonism sinks away; here the apostle arrives at things that the entire Greek world had never suspected, speaking as he does like someone who knows, who has a commission, who has seen this one God himself with his own eyes.

The trained ears on the Areopagus, as they take in this speech, will by turns have been struck by the familiarity and the freshness of all these things. The words were familiar, to be sure, but what was so fresh about them was that here they were being applied to a living God and not to a lifeless concept, to a God who is Lord of all and not to an impersonal indwelling Force. That was the shocking, revolutionary nature of Paul's words. Everything he was going to say next, no matter how much it seemed to resemble what Greek thinkers had dreamed up about their *Logos*, their "World Reason," was absolutely and totally different from what had ever entered the hearts of pagans. Standing between the noblest expressions of Plato and the Stoics on the one hand, and the Mars Hill speech on the other, is the confession of God as Lord of all, the Almighty ruler of our lives.

Verses 26 and 27 next deal separately with the world of man and its relation to God. Paul sees this human world as a unit, leaving aside the distinction between nations and races. He does this not so much to echo Stoic thought but because Scripture itself is very clear about the unity of the human race. This confession of the unity of mankind at once delivers a death blow to the existence of national religions in the old pagan sense. That is why this sermon of Paul's is still so valuable for the mission field: in one blow it shatters the old faith in the divine nature of the tribe or nation and reduces the significance of the national element to its proper proportions. Paul shows how the wise dispensation of the living God governs the allotted periods and boundaries of the different nations, and that this arrangement has no other goal than that they should seek God, in the hope of feeling their way toward Him and finding Him. It does not say that the pagans have actually sought God; all it says is that this was God's goal and purpose in dealing with them. To the extent that there is talk of seeking God, that seeking is purely and solely a fruit of God's dealing with them and of God's care for them.

The verb "to feel" that Paul used here contains perhaps a gentle hint at the degeneration that this "seeking" had led to in the pagan world. They had wanted to "feel" God in the physical sense of the word, to touch an image of God with their fingers. Then this desire "to feel" implies that in their hands God's purpose with them, actively present in the life of all mankind, had been perverted—had been turned into a search for some sensory thing, something physical that they could touch. Everything that had come from God, as soon as it entered the sphere of man, had become polluted and defiled, resulting in a self-willed invention of gods, with the desire to be able to touch them.

In the verses 28 and 29 the apostle next quotes some words from Greek poets. Originally, of course, those poets meant something else by them. Paul does not speak of the "divine being," of Zeus, of the Logos, of the god of the philosophers;

he is talking about the living God who has appeared in Christ. Still, it is true about the living God what the Stoics thought about their divine being. Only, everything is different, because God is different. With subtle irony Paul brings out that those Greek poets, despite their fine and profound words, never issued a flaming protest against the worship of images made of silver or stone; on the contrary, they tolerated it, or with philosophical hauteur humored it. That was because their gods are different from the only true God. They did at times express fine thoughts and lovely ideas about the relation between God and world, but they always had it wrong because the God they taught was an "unknown god," not the living God, the God of Jesus Christ. Is Paul here flattering pagan philosophy? Not at all! What he is doing is challenging the pagan intellectuals to expose the century-old idol worship in its folly, showing at the same time that idol worship survived in spite of all their philosophical reflections, because the God of the philosophers, too, is an "unknown god."

All this is clarified further in verses 30 and 31. After all, that is where the philosophers just quoted are included in the "times of ignorance." They knew a little more than the common people, but they did not really know God either. They too were ignorant, and their ignorance too was culpable ignorance. They too were called to repent in view of the coming Day of Judgment. Neither Socrates, nor Plato, nor Aratus, nor any other thinker in Antiquity had ever summoned people to *metanoia*, to repentance, to genuine conversion. They did at times berate their age for its folly, but they never understood that it dishonored God. They never in God's name fulminated against sin. All of a sudden what is heard here, as the conclusion of a discourse into which all kinds of citations from these intellectuals are appropriately interwoven, is a loud and clear summons to repent. That is possible here, because all this time there was another God, the God who made the world and everything in it. The command to repent is not a Jewish label stuck onto a Hellenistic speech (thus Dibelius), but it is the moral as well as the logical consequence of a discourse in which an assortment of Stoic words are used but in which every idea was different from what Stoicism taught.

Concluding observations

Three closing comments can still be made about the nature of the speech on Mars Hill and about how it ended.

My first comment is the thought that Paul in this speech teaches very clearly that God is immanent in all that He has created. He cites with approval the word of the pagan poet who had written that "*in him we live and move and have our being.*" Very well, according to many philologists and theologians, this idea is indeed Stoic and pagan, not Christian. Albert Schweitzer here locates the deep gulf that separates the mysticism of the Stoics and the "Christ mysticism" of Paul. Is he right?

We should first note that the idea of God's indwelling in all of creation is assuredly biblical. It is God who "*gives life to all*" (Neh. 9:6).[78] "*When you send forth your Spirit, they are created, and you renew the face of the ground*" (Ps. 104:30). God upholds all things "*by the word of his power*" (Heb. 1:3). Found throughout the Bible is the idea that God is not only the cause of the origin of the world, but also that this world from moment to moment is sustained by Him and "exists in Him."[79] Thus the word Paul used on this occasion is not a new sound in the whole of revelation, but they link up on all sides with what had already been expressed in other forms as well.

Much depends on what you understand by the preposition *in*. "*In him we live and move and have our being.*" The Greek preposition *en* that is translated by "in" is extremely difficult to translate. It is infinitely richer than our "in." It can mean "in the sphere of" or "in communion with," but it can also be used with the meaning "by virtue of."[80] In the present context we would be wise not to lean too heavily on it, but instead to leave room for the subtle nuances that are possible here. When it says in the Epistles that the believer is "in" Christ, then the word "in" has a different meaning than in the Areopagus speech. At any rate, it is nonsense to brand this statement as pantheistic: the entire context in which it appears definitely precludes any implication of pantheism.

A second comment is in order about the abrupt ending of the speech. Just as Paul begins to talk about resurrection from the dead, the intellectual sophisticates of Athens call him to order and cut him off. To our way of thinking there

---

[78] [The *Statenvertaling* quoted here reads: "*en Gij maakt die allen levend,*" thus as in the Septuagint, which reads: "*and thou quickenest them all.*" KJV has: "and thou preservest them all." Cf. some modern English translations of Neh. 9:6: "You alone are the LORD who made the heavens, the earth, and the seas and all that is in them, *and you preserve all of them . . .*" (ESV); ". . . *You give life to everything*" (NIV).]

[79] Kirsopp Lake, *The Beginnings of Christianity*, vol. IV, note at vs. 28.

[80] See Kittel, *Theologisches Wörterbuch zum Neuen Testament*, s.v. en.

is something tragic about that; after all, the resurrection from the dead seemed to have been mentioned only casually. Upon further reflection, however, the case is not quite what we are inclined to think at first blush.

Paul's discourse could not do without Christ's resurrection as a sign of his divine appointment as Judge of the world. This had to be emphasized in order to prepare for the gospel of the Cross and the grace that we may receive from His hand. It also had to be explicated in order to bring into sharp relief the difference between the gospel and pagan thought. The Greek world in the Hellenistic age was inclined to view death as the release of the divine soul from the shackles of the body and thus as a unification with the divine being. Images are still extant that depict the moment when the divine soul, the *daimon* that lives in man, escapes from its prison and ascends to heaven. In the pantheism of the time this idea was a necessary ingredient, as it is to this day in various Asiatic worldviews. Nowhere else is the contrast between the gospel and paganism more apparent than precisely in the doctrine of the Resurrection. That doctrine, after all, stamps man as a creature, even in death and after death. He is not absorbed into the All, he does not vanish into the divine All-being. He remains a human being. The doctrine of the Resurrection makes the boundary line between Creature and creation into a definitive line, into a permanent boundary. Once Paul has spoken about the relation of God and man, he cannot remain silent about the Resurrection. He must bring out the logical conclusion of his speech, even though he knows that the simple words "raised from the dead" clashed with the thinking of the age. He must have steered toward that moment with great care and even with pastoral tenderness, but he was not allowed to spare these Athenian intellectuals. Hence it is no coincidence that this phrase called up resistance. We ought to assume, rather, that those philosophically trained hearers on the Areopagus listened with growing astonishment to the beginning of Paul's discourse and kept asking themselves how it was that this speaker was saying old things that were nevertheless new. Not until they heard the words "raised from the dead" did they realize the deep gulf between their own thinking and what this preacher meant. Thus, the speech on Mars Hill came to a natural end; it broke off abruptly where it had to break off, where the contrast was fully demonstrated. Paul did everything within his power to slowly prepare the hearts of his audience for the great new things he had to share, but the thread of his entire argument finally forced him to say without hesitation what he was not allowed to keep back.

So then, did the speech on Mars Hill, however tactfully and carefully delivered, end up being a failure? No, not at all! Anybody who has ever had to contend for the gospel before the kind of audience as on Mars Hill, and who knows how immensely difficult it is to convince such jaded ears, cannot read the close of this account without feeling shamed. There is something of jubilation in Luke's voice as he ends his report of this event: "*But some men joined him and believed, among whom also were Dionysius the Areopagite and a woman named Damaris and others with them*" (vs. 34). Such a response to a speech, made under such difficult circumstances, is amazing. It is easier to speak to savages and cannibals, or to tax collectors and prostitutes, than to worshippers of rhetorical form and jaded know-it-alls like those men of Athens. Paul ventured to preach to them, and his fearless faith was not without fruit.

Summary

When we sum up all of the above it becomes apparent that the speech on Mars Hill has often been misunderstood. The Apologetic Fathers of the Early Church read more into it than Paul intended; they interpreted the central portion of the speech too much apart from the beginning and the end. Paul does not endorse Greek thought; he does not talk about an All-being but about the living God, and he ends with a call to repentance. All statements in between ought to be read in light of the beginning and the end. Then it also becomes clear that the gulf between Stoicism and gospel is not concealed, but that every word Paul uses, given the context, acquires a new content. Stoic ideas take on new meaning once he applies them to the living God. Man in his sinful dreams about the gods he has invented may sometimes have said things that are true about the one and only true God who appeared in Christ. Intuitions like that can create the impression that they are born of the Spirit, and I would not want to deny that the Spirit of God has worked among the pagans more than we often suppose. But then we must add at once that even the most beautiful statements, such as those we come across in the holy books of China and India and Japan and other countries, in the sense intended by those who produced them, have no other meaning than apostasy from God. They exchanged the truth about

God for a lie by applying that truth to what they called God, to their fantasized God, the unknown God.

In Paul's discourse on Mars Hill we have a model of a missional sermon. That does not mean that we should preach exactly the same way always and everywhere. It does mean that we have to wrestle everywhere with the same questions, with the same paganism that sometimes breaks out in beautiful and profound language about the relation between God and man. It also means that we ought to profit from what God wants to teach us in this sermon.

Here we stand, with the message of Christ, in a world that is searching, that is seeking in the hope of finding, a world that has already thought and said so much about divine things. We may not hide the gulf that separates pagan beliefs from what God has revealed; we may not cover up the contrasts; we are to draw the lines with clarity and precision. However, we must do so with care and do so with love. To repel is easy; to flatter is also easy; but to combat with empathy, to witness with conviction, that is hard. The ambassador of Christ can do this only if living in him is the same Spirit that will "*convict the world concerning sin and righteousness and judgment.*"

6. The Young Church in a Pagan World

Church and world

When a young church on the mission field begins to grow, she is immediately confronted with a precarious situation. The world in which she lives is in no way prepared to tolerate such a church in its midst. On all sides, strong resistance arises that wants to hamper the growth of the young plant. The political and social relations around her have evolved from a totally different worldview and hence are not at all suited for the life of the Church. Yet there is not a chance that this young church will be able in the short term to bring about any change. She will have to grow and develop under a regime of all kinds of rules and relationships that are at odds with her own inner life. As for education, particularly higher education, all of it is in the hands of other powers, and for the time being no changes will be possible there either. In short, the Church must find her way in a world which operates on the basis of other fundamental principles and which therefore attempts—and must attempt—to thwart and frustrate the Church without letup.

It's in the nature of the case. Today, too, we face these phenomena in all those countries where the gospel is beginning to gain firmer ground: in India, China, Japan, and many more countries. Initially, such a non-Christian world can do little else than view the new faith as a "*religio illicita*," a religious creed that is not officially recognized and also, in effect, not tolerated. Such a world must do so because it is not a neutral, colorless whole that has room for all kinds of spiritual currents and movements. It is, rather, a living organism which by virtue of its own internal laws must exclude whatever is at odds with its essence. A non-Christian world like that is held together by certain religious convictions and by all sorts of mores and customs which over centuries have evolved in tandem with those religious convictions. In every respect, therefore, such a world is of a clearly defined type. For precisely this reason the new arrival in religion is experienced as unbelief, as a violation of ancestral customs, as a dissolution of state and nation.

This is even more true when the young church is born in a country where the old paganism is still in its full strength, where it is still the cement of the entire life of the people. Here every power immediately braces itself to prevent the foreign faith from making any progress. A powerful tension develops between the Church and the general population, a tension that cannot but occasion continually fresh conflicts. In the long run, only two things can then really happen. It can happen that the Church, despite all opposition, nevertheless gradually begins to pervade all of life, until at last she becomes as it were the binding force that holds everything together, the living power that governs every social and economic institution and gives it a new direction. What can also happen is that the life of the nation itself begins to develop into a different type, that it loses some of its old, all-encompassing power and is transformed into a less defined whole in which there is room for a diversity of religions and spiritual directions and where only common traditions and ethnic identity make up the binding forces that maintain a measure of equilibrium.

Our Western society in the course of centuries has increasingly acquired the characteristics of the second type. It is no longer borne up by a common world-and-life view but admits all views. The atheist can live quietly and peaceably alongside the committed Christian and the confirmed communist can live next door to the dyed-in-the wool conservative without the two harming each other. Western countries have room for all; everybody can live their lives according to their own convictions. What binds people together is not any religious belief but only national solidarity, a quantity that cannot be weighed or measured. That said, we must not forget that this condition cannot in any respect be considered normal. It evolved slowly in Europe, as the outcome of all kinds of intellectual and spiritual movements and currents: Catholicism and Reformation, Humanism and Enlightenment, and many more. We can never expect such conditions on the mission field, for here every society has the instinctive impulse to put up a fierce resistance against any and all forces that might destroy the inner unity. This explains why everywhere on today's mission field the tension between Church and Nation is beginning to take on the aspect of a looming threat, a growing danger for the Church.

When we look at the Early Church from this vantage point, it cannot escape us that she came to manifestation in exceptional circumstances. As we saw above, the strong national ties had grown weak; a humane, cosmopolitan spirit set the tone throughout the Greco-Roman world. The forces of resistance to the gospel were not as fierce as they often are. This world did offer room for a diversity of religious persuasions.

Still, even here all sorts of tensions soon surfaced. The social institutions of that world—think of slavery, of marital relationships—had evolved under the sway of ancient pagan conceptions, and these institutions had survived despite the fact that paganism itself threatened to perish through senile decay. Everywhere in the provinces the old, national institutions were still operative and strong. The old pagan religion still had a hold on the whole of society. Even where beliefs and convictions were already beginning to wane, people still took pride in observing the old religious customs; even mockers and atheists dared not neglect them. Furthermore, special difficulties arose in connection with the Roman Empire, that big tent which housed the many nations, personified in the person of the deified emperor.

So even though conditions were relatively favourable, at least when compared to what we experience on the various mission fields today, we must not for one moment assume that the ancient world made room for the Church. The Church had to struggle to gain a foothold here as well. She had to find her way in a maze of currents and phenomena that were in conflict with her essence. Here too she had to face down enmity and hatred, for the sake of the Name of Christ, her King.

The missionary mandate that the Saviour gave his apostles before his departure contains these remarkable words: "*teaching them to observe all that I have commanded you*" (Matt. 28:20a). Thus, Jesus himself already pointed out that preaching the gospel, even administering baptism, did not end the apostles' task. They next had to teach these young Christians, in the world of their day, in their national contexts, to observe all that Christ had commanded them. It is worth noting that it does not say: "teach them all that I have commanded you." That would have been a relatively easy task, a task of regular catechism, of ongoing instruction. The words "teaching them *to observe*" entail much more than that. They imply the necessity of pedagogical tact, of pastoral wisdom and caution. What matters is to gradually accustom the feet of young and inexperienced Christians to walking the path of peace. That may require at one time to be very tolerant, at other times to be very strict. It may be necessary to roll out the missionary mandate slowly and carefully, lest hasty instruction harm the natural growth of the Christian life. Those few words entrusted the circle of the apostles with the calling of educating the Church in relation to the countless difficulties that would be occasioned by the daily friction with the surrounding world. And so we also see Paul traversing the lands not only as a preacher of the gospel but also as a wise father leading his young children in the faith from milk to solid food, from the basic principles to their natural applications.

Shaping congregational life

The apostle Paul paid crucial attention to the issue of educating the local church. For the young Christians, life in the Church was at the same time a replacement of life in the national community. They had been cut loose from the anchors of ancient customs and in a certain sense now faced the task, in unison and intimate bonds with each other and the Word, of creating new customs. Of critical importance was the manner in which this was done.

The first thing that strikes us is that Paul as a rule has a congregation perform as a unit. The Book of Acts reports on numerous meetings of a church as a body. These assemblies discussed all kinds of matters which among us today would be handled by the local council, session, or consistory. Even prior to the Pauline period we hear of such congregational meetings, and Paul honored this usage everywhere. Upon their return to Antioch from the first missionary journey, Paul and his companions "*gathered the church together*" (Acts 14:27) where they reported on what they had experienced in the field. When shortly thereafter in the same church of Antioch a dispute arose concerning circumcision, Paul and a few others were appointed, again in a church gathering, to travel to Jerusalem to seek the advice of the apostles and elders (Acts 15:1–3). In Jerusalem they were again received in a gathering of the whole church, where they related "*all that God had done with them*" (Acts 15:4). And so the earliest history of the Church advanced from church gathering to church gathering. Paul wrote his letters to specific churches; they were intended to be read in the church at its very next gathering. We hear very little about specific tasks for a local council or consistory.

None of this is strange. In the mission field a church gathering is an institution of the utmost importance. All sorts of questions concerning the social and cultural environment have to be discussed by the congregation. In his intriguing book on missions in New Guinea, Christian Keysser writes that these gatherings really function for all the Papuan believers as the primary source of information.

> Whatever occupies the local church is discussed in these gatherings. They provide a wealth of experience and education. People share at great length what each knows about social and economic issues, for these all play a significant role in their daily lives.[81]

In former days, the community, with its fixed customs, had enough guidelines for regulating the whole of their lives, but now that they were expelled, as it were, from the old pagan community, everything had to be created anew in terms of the new faith, and that had to be done together, engaging every member. In regions of British India where mass conversions to Christianity have taken place, the same need is felt to come together on a regular basis, preferably every evening, for the purpose of praying and communally discussing the ramifications of the new-found faith for everyday life.[82] All this is perfectly natural, and it was to be expected that the Early Church would fully realize these things as well.

Worthy of note as well is that the sensitive and difficult cases of mutual discipline are also discussed in meetings of the whole congregation. Paul has no compunctions about touching on it in his epistles to the churches. In a young church, disciplinary matters are extremely important because it is to be expected that the leaven of the old life does not immediately lose its effectiveness. In churches on the mission field, accordingly, one often runs into all kinds of problems—questionable Christian conduct that must be treated firmly but also cautiously. A close study of the Pauline epistles will lead to the conclusion that the apostle applied the remedy of discipline only sporadically. Serious cases of abuse are mentioned by him without immediately pointing out that the exercise of discipline is in order. Again, this is only natural. The young church must first have her conscience formed and educated by God's Word before it can exercise discipline. It may well be possible to pressure her, prematurely and from the outside, to exercise discipline without delay, but if that discipline is applied apart from her conscience, it all too easily degenerates in pharisaical formalism.

---

[81] Chr. Keysser, *Eine Papuagemeinde* (Kassel: Bärenreiter-Verlag, 1929), p. 34.

[82] J. W. Pickett, *Christian Mass Movements in India* (New York and Cincinnati: Abingdon Press, 1933), p. 136.

In those passages where Paul writes about discipline, he sees it as a conscious act of the whole church. In the serious and offensive case described in 1 Corinthians 5, Paul wants the whole church to be filled with mourning, in order that the offender "*be removed from among you*" (1 Cor. 5:2). The same mourning is also to be at the basis of the "shunning" of those persons who ask foolish questions and quarrel about the law in order to try and split the church. Against such people as well, the church must take a firm stand, united in holy mourning.[83] The church is to shun all these aberrant brothers. She is not to associate with them but avoid them. This shunning should not arise from arrogance or pharisaism but from love, and it should have as its goal that those brothers feel ashamed and repent (2 Thess. 3:6, 14). In other words, to be able to exercise strong discipline it is not enough that a church possesses a Word of God in which a particular sin is clearly branded a sin, but it is also essential that the conscience of that church, guided by God's Word, has advanced to such a level that the church as a whole can be filled with mourning about the sin and can admonish the sinner in holy anger. If one wishes a church to practice discipline too early and too artificially, the danger is great of fostering legalism and pharisaism. All churches on the mission field, from their earliest days right to the present day, are prone to lapse into a type of nomism, a fixation on rules and precepts, and in connection with that a form of purely outward discipline. By virtue of their very nature, pagan religions are totalitarian: they provide a system of hard-and-fast norms and customs that everyone is held to. When people turn from paganism to faith in Christ, they very much want to see this new religion, too, as totalitarian. That is to say, they expect from Christianity a rigorous system of norms and rules, equal to the system they were used to. This stubborn inclination must always be resisted because it fails to appreciate the seriousness of personal moral decisions, fails to see the role of the believers' conscience, and fails to protect the Christian life from turning into a dry and dull system of rigorous rules.

For mutual discipline the Early Church had an excellent tool in the so-called house churches. They are mentioned four times in Scripture; the one in Ephesus at the home of Aquila and Priscilla, one in Rome at the same couple's home, one in Laodicea, and one in Colossae (1 Cor. 16:19, Rom. 16:5, Col. 4:15, Phil.

---

[83] See A. M. Brouwer, *De kerkorganisatie der eerste eeuw en wij*, p. 98.

4:22). Unfortunately, we know very little about these house churches. No doubt they had their own organization of sorts and their own distinct leaders. Such intimate house churches could of course do greater justice to the institution of mutual discipline than could the larger churches. We also do not know how a house church was involved in the wider local church, so that we can form only a poor picture of how they functioned. Most likely, they made for a close link between a young growing church and family life, including the domestic slaves.[84]

As we trace how Paul formed the conscience of the Church, it strikes us that he would tackle any question in depth, not just in passing. This is significant enough to merit close attention. The Christian life in the world is never discussed by Paul in a totalitarian but always in a radical sense—down to the roots. He does not give a host of rules to blanket life, but every time again he draws a line from the periphery to the center and in this way teaches young Christians to view every problem by starting from Christ, taking their point of departure from Him. He seeks to awaken people's conscience in terms of the faith. Paul wants to foster a Christian mind and a Christian mode of conduct in which everything is viewed from the fundamentals of faith in Christ. That is a much harder and more time-consuming task than giving a long string of precepts, but it is more useful and most essential for arming the Church against any spirit of nomism, legalism, and formalism.

To give just a few examples, think first of all of the exceptionally weighty and comprehensive question of circumcision. We discussed its seriousness above, in chapter 1. One needs to read a letter like the one to the Galatians to see how thoroughly the apostle tackles the question. When a Christian who was a pagan has himself circumcised, it means that he allows himself to be incorporated into Israel as a nation; that he grasps at the all-encompassing regimen of the law that bore Israel's existence as a people; that he looks for his justification in that law; that he does not see that the new phase in the history of Divine Revelation is a phase in which we are gifted with freedom in Christ. It means that he is letting go of Christ and taking refuge in the old things that have passed away (see Gal. 5: 2–6). Following this train of thought carefully, we sense that the apostle does not want to dismiss these difficult questions with a few dogmatic slogans but

[84] Ibid., pp. 52ff. See also P. A. E. Sillevis Smit, *De organisatie van de Christelijke Kerk in den apostolischen tijd* [The organization of the Christian Church in apostolic times] (Rotterdam: T. de Vries, 1910), pp. 65, 113–114.

instead delves into an issue like this until he encounters Christ. It is the apostle's earnest endeavour to demonstrate to this church (which is so prone to error) how she can find the answer in Christ himself. He wants to teach her to think and live starting from Christ. And that is radical.

A second example we would like to mention here is that of marriage. Marriage is a problem on all mission fields because non-Christian religions view marriage in a totally different way from how it is taught in God's Word. Consequently, pagans surround marriage with completely different moral rules. The world in which Paul laboured seesawed between asceticism contemptuous of marriage and sexual immorality ruinous of marriage. The Hellenistic world in both its religious currents and philosophical schools displayed a strong tendency toward asceticism, hence failed to appreciate the spiritual value of marriage.[85] At the same time, life in those days exhibited a moral decadence that was horrendous (cf. Rom. 1:18ff). For that very reason the question of marriage was a crucial issue for the young Church. That serious problems were present in the Church herself is evident from the first letter to the Corinthians. Now then, it is remarkable that this big problem, too, is tackled by Paul in a radical way. He starts with Christ; he shows how the bond of Christ to his Church is really the profound reality of which the marital bond between husband and wife has been given to us as a shadow (Eph. 5:22–33). New light is cast on all the concrete issues related to marriage: they are examined and experienced in a new, Christian way, and the answers are looked for in terms of the fundamentals of the faith.[86]

Our third example is the regular collections. This practice, too, is not without significance in a mission church. Pagan religions are by nature expensive; they require a lot of money for feasts and sacrifices and processions. Christian worship is sober, hence much less costly. On the island of Bali there were sometimes people who felt attracted to the Christian faith for no other reason than its low cost. In cases like that it is imperative to make clear to young Christians that the Christian faith cannot but be costly: it demands everything

[85] See M. Hansen, *Het ascetisme en Paulus' verkondiging van het nieuwe leven* [Asceticism and Paul's proclamation of the new life] (Th.D. diss.; Zutphen: Ruys, 1939), pp. 21–32.

[86] Th. Delleman, *Het huwelijksvraagstuk in 1 Cor. VII* (Aalten: De Graafschap, 1933).

from a person, also material gifts and contributions. When Paul comes to talk about the regular collections he does not hesitate to devote several chapters of his letter to the topic (2 Cor. 8 and 9). He again approaches the subject in a radical way. He does not utter authoritative statements to dictate behavior. He even states emphatically that he does not want to "*command*" this "*act of grace.*" Instead, he points to Christ, who "*though he was rich yet for your sake became poor, so that by his poverty you might become rich*" (2 Cor. 8:7–9). Seen in that light, every collection becomes a great and wonderful thing: it is a humble and thankful service to Him who gave himself for us. The apostle taught his disciples to think along these lines when dealing with the many concrete questions they faced.

The Church and social and political relations

The idea of a neutral state is unknown among heathen nations; the state is a religiously sanctioned institution that receives its splendor and authority from religion. In Paul's days, as we have seen, national and ethnic ties had been robbed of their ancient glory and much of the sacral character of folk customs had been lost. Nevertheless, many usages and conventions were still acknowledged as godly and holy, and therefore as inviolable. In addition, divine status and dignity was ascribed to the Roman Empire as it embraced many nations.

In the initial stage, it seemed that the contact of the Christian religion with the political powers of the time would not meet with many objections. The Roman rulers of the world had a strong sense of justice, with the result that serious clashes could be avoided. The Early Church valued this from the outset and expressed its heartfelt appreciation of it. Paul in his letters more than once borrows rules from Roman civil law in order to illustrate various facets of the faith.[87] For example, he uses images borrowed from Roman succession law, from adoption law, and so on. Generally speaking, the Early Church appreciated the Roman legal system as a blessing for the world, since it was based on principles of morality and equity. Calvin too acknowledged the blessings of the Roman

---

[87] V. H. Rutgers, *De invloed van het Christendom op het Romeinsche recht* [The influence of Christianity on Roman law] (Amsterdam: Bakker, 1940). [Professor Rutgers read this paper in a public meeting celebrating the 60th founding day of the Free University, 21 Oct. 1940, thus a few months after Germany conquered his country and imposed its regime of Nazi law and order.]

legal system: once, while discussing the seventh commandment, he remarked that the Roman laws accord so well with the order instituted by God that it almost seems "as if the authors of those laws had learned from Moses what decency requires and what agrees with nature."[88]

All this is true in particular of civil law, the body of laws that governs the legal relations between citizens. But also in the whole field of criminal law the early Christians could only respect and obey Roman authority. In the Gospels and in Acts, Roman procurators (governors of provinces) function as the authorities that uphold and maintain what is just and fair. To be sure, they were usually no match for the intrigues of the Jewish Sanhedrin, yet that does not take away from the unmistakable fact that they had people's interests very much at heart. Especially the humble town clerk of Ephesus proved that the lawful interests of citizens were in safe hands (Acts 19:35–41). Thus it was quite in agreement with the factual situation when Paul wrote in Romans chapter 13 that the governing authorities were "*not a terror to good conduct, but to bad,*" and that "*he who does good receives their approval.*" The Christian church had the enormous privilege of being able to grow and develop in a world in which law and order was held in high regard.

The situation turned more problematic the moment the interests of the empire were at stake. However tolerant Roman governance was of all religious schools and currents, it became highly intolerant when it came to the divinity of the emperor. Roman imperialism contained elements which sooner or later had to lead to a mortal struggle with the Church. In Acts we still meet very few symptoms of the growing tension between Church and Empire. In the epistles, however, especially in the later ones, there is mounting evidence of conflict with the religious subtext of empire. In his second letter to Timothy, Paul writes from Rome that at his trial in the imperial court he was rescued by God's grace from the "lion's mouth" (4:17).

As for social relations, here the Church could at first hardly make a dent. The institution of slavery was so deeply entrenched in that society that it was impossible to overturn it in one stroke. Paul's letters do not give us any fundamental reflections on slavery, but they do indicate how master and slave ought to conduct themselves by Christian standards. Paul provides guidelines in the short

[88] Quoted in Rutgers, ibid., p. 21 [from *Calvini Opera*, 24:689].

epistle to Philemon and with various expressions in the other epistles (e.g., Eph. 6:3–8). And again, he does this in a radical way, starting from Christ. As a social institution slavery itself did remain intact, to be sure, but internally it was changed and renewed so completely that virtually only the name survived. Thus, the social institutions themselves were not attacked, but life within their frameworks was altered from the bottom up.

The same is true of the position of women. In the age of Hellenism there were schools of thought that wanted to put women somewhat on a par with men and give her equal status, but there were other schools that wanted women to have only very limited rights. Paul says very little about the rights of women, but we notice that he credits them with playing an honorable role in the life of the Church. The Early Church called women to all sorts of *diakonia* (service). Again, we know too little of those times to be able to say with certainty what the position was of Phoebe, the deaconess of the church in Cenchreae (Rom. 16:1), or what the work was of the widows of age 60 and above about whose role the apostle gives advice (1 Tim. 5:9ff). Yet it is certain that sisters like Phoebe, Priscilla (mentioned first in Rom. 16:3, before her husband), Tryphaena and Tryphosa (Rom. 16:12) enjoyed great respect and honor. In this way the question of the position of women was resolved in principle, not by devising all kinds of theories, but by starting from Christ.

Accordingly, the young church could not immediately act in a holistic manner. She could not attack the whole of life in society in all its terrains and branches but had to grow up amid relationships that had evolved out of other worldviews. She was able, however, to proceed in a radical way: that is to say, she could reveal a new form of life, a form of life which in the long run would cause the old forms to implode. The gospel did not begin at once to work in a revolutionary way; initially it seemed to acquiesce in conditions such as they were, but within the framework of those conditions it awakened new forces and new possibilities which would, with the passing of the years or centuries, give shape to a new society.

The Church and her relation to her pagan surroundings

The most difficult problems for the Church occurred, of course, when facing customs and usages which not only had evolved from another worldview, but which also clearly displayed their pagan character. Then there would be no question of tolerating the old, but the Church had to intervene and protest immediately.

In what we are accustomed to calling a "primitive" society, all public acts are steeped in religion. Whether one is building a house or planting a crop, marrying off one's daughter or conducting a funeral, all these acts in one way or another are intimately connected with the religious fundamentals of life and will therefore be accompanied by ritual acts of various description. However, that had not been the case for a long time in the world where Paul was working. That world was already to a considerable degree secularized. Paganism was drained and worn out. Religion had been pushed back to a much more restricted area than it had covered in former times. Still, that does not alter the fact that in Paul's days countless religious precepts were still being observed.

The problem faced by the first Christians was all the more daunting to the degree in which they did not give up their place in society. Erastus, the city treasurer of Corinth, calmly stayed in his post even after he became a Christian. Other Christians too kept their prominent positions in society after their conversion. But precisely these high-placed Christians, in the nature of the case, more than once had to participate in public ceremonies that involved sacral acts, sacrifices to gods, and so on.[89] How they found their way amid the many conflicts of conscience that they inevitably had to deal with is not known; we do admire their courage for staying in their post, even though that post brought them into the gravest dangers.

What was true for prominent Christians on a large scale was of course just as true on a smaller scale for women who were married to pagan husbands or for slaves who were in the service of pagan masters. They could be compelled at any moment to participate in pagan rituals that they were duty-bound to abhor and condemn. Their husbands or masters were not always willing to respect their conscientious scruples, and this would often result in persecution within the household that could turn into real torment. The letters of Peter (especially 1 Peter 2:18–3:7) allude several times to such extremely painful situations.

Of all the many issues that arose in this area, the one that is most often mentioned in Paul's letters is the eating of meat that had originally been offered to

---

[89] [Cf. 2 Kings 5:19.]

idols. This certainly belonged to the thorniest questions that the first Christians had to deal with.

There is a custom among all heathen nations that an animal may not be slaughtered except in relation to the gods. Killing an animal, destroying life, is such a critical act that people dare not do it solely for their own benefit. As a rule, therefore, heathens do not butcher apart from religious ritual; they butcher after an invocation of divine powers and in a relationship with those powers. But once an animal has been slaughtered and a certain portion offered to the gods, the remaining meat may be eaten. By eating it, a person is really eating meat that belongs to the gods, meat that was dedicated to the gods, and eating it places a person in an intimate relationship with the gods. Thus, both the butchering and the eating were sacral acts. Now it is true that these customs had already been relaxed in the Greco-Roman world. Nevertheless, much of the meat that was sold in the marketplace came from the temple and had therefore been sacrificial meat. Accordingly, time and again the difficult question arose whether Christians were allowed to eat such meat. Would they not burden their conscience by it and deny their Lord?

This issue became considerably more difficult in Corinth by the fact that there was a small circle in the church who claimed to be more "enlightened," to possess "knowledge." They called themselves the strong ones; they had determined that idols don't exist and that therefore all so-called sacral meat was nothing but ordinary meat. It was not possible to enter objectively into a relationship with the gods, since those gods after all did not exist. All idol worship was a lie and idle fantasy. So far so good. By contrast, however, there were those in the church of Corinth who did not believe eating sacrificial meat was all that innocent. They felt that the enchanting power of the old pagan beliefs was still far too strong in their heart that they could not help being offended when seeing their fellow Christians sitting down at sacrificial meals, ostensibly with a clear conscience.

Once again, Paul dealt with this thorny issue in accordance with his tried-and-true method: *radically*, starting from what lay at the root of the issue. In his first letter to the Corinthians, we see him admonishing the "strong" in chapter 8 and addressing the "weak" in chapter 10. One can indeed state that, objectively speaking, idols don't exist, and such a statement is then not untrue. Yet that does not resolve this delicate question. What is objectively true cannot be the only criterion; equally important are the subjective feelings that linger deep in people's hearts. When the heart is still under the spell of the old pagan religion, then everything that puts one in touch again with those idols is as it were a phenomenon of demonic magnetism; then the soul is once more ensnared in sin. To this extent it can be said that to sacrifice to the gods is to sacrifice to demons (1 Cor. 10:20). Hence there are many more considerations that must decide the issue. The Corinthian church must not dissolve into a party of the strong and a party of the weak. She must seek the right path forward, starting from the gospel of Christ. And so Paul offers some personal guidelines for how to proceed, in a concerted effort to keep the holiness and the unity of the church intact.

Questions about faith

Of course, there were not only questions of daily living that needed to be dealt with; the churches were also preoccupied with all sorts of questions about faith. These too are discussed by the apostle in his letters, and here too he goes about it in a radical way.

When we read those letters, they sometimes leave us with the impression that they deal with abstract dogmas. A more careful reading, however, should convince us at once that almost all of these letters were written in connection with very concrete issues that preoccupied the churches. Many a beautiful chapter in I Corinthians we owe to a letter containing many questions that the church of Corinth had first written to Paul about. In his reply, the apostle treats each question separately, and in his hands each one becomes grand and profound. He never dwells on the trivial or the incidental, but always digs deep, going down to the roots. Whether he talks about marriage, or the Lord's supper, or ordinary church gatherings, or resurrection from the dead—with each issue he puts the spotlight on the great work of Christ and from there he gives his answer.

To a case of rivalry and dissension in Philippi we owe one of the most beautiful chapters in the Pauline epistles: the hymn of praise in honor of Christ "*who humbled himself by being obedient to the point of death*," wherefore God highly exalted him (Phil. 2:5–11). Again, when some Christians had spoken ill of him for being so ordinary and mundane and for being unable to share any visions and heavenly experiences, it became an occasion for Paul to write one of the most moving passages ever written: his "boast" about what Christ had shown him, namely, that His power "*is made perfect in weakness*" (2 Cor. 12:1–10). The smallest question put to him, every comment made about him, brought him to deep thoughts, forced him to open his eyes to the great works of God, showed him visions of sublime loftiness, and so caused all things to be viewed in the light of eternity.

That is how this apostle, driven by the Holy Spirit, taught this early church "*to observe all that I have commanded you.*" Not by holding before them rule upon rule and commandment upon commandment, not by answering all their puny questions and minor difficulties, but by always bringing them back to the source and by teaching them to view everything starting from Christ.

Reading through the letters of Paul to the various churches and to individuals, we are astonished by the great variety of opinions and problems he had to deal with. The letter to the Romans confronts us with the great question of Judaism in all its multiple facets. Discussed are law and grace, the righteousness that comes by faith, and the obedience that flows from fellowship with Christ. The later chapters show something of the great plan that God had with the world, the plan whereby the apostasy of Israel was made to serve as a blessing for the nations.

The letter to the Colossians acquaints us with entirely different issues again. There the apostle faces the grim monster of syncretism that was stretching out its dangerous claws to the young church. Paul wrestles with the peril of mixing faith in Christ with remnants of pagan ideas. He fights a battle against the spirit of pantheistic mysticism, of world-flight, of the speculative theosophy so characteristic of Hellenism.

The letters to Timothy and Titus plunge us into questions about organizing the life of a church. They deal with discipline, and the calling of elders, and all manner of practical issues.

Indeed, it is a broad range of ideas that the apostle covers. With his readers he traverses all the domains of contemporary life and thought, and at every step he shows that in Christ all things have become new. He who has seen the Cross on which the Saviour died—once a person has accepted Him as his Lord and Saviour—to him a world of surprises opens up. Life changes, marriage changes, one's position in society changes, relations change with people under you and over you, masters and slaves—in short, all things are changed and renewed. "*I have been crucified with Christ. It is no longer I who live, but Christ who lives in me. And the life I now live in the flesh I live by faith in the Son of God, who loved me and gave himself for me*" (Gal. 2:20).

As he deals with all these questions, the apostle betrays deep emotion. There are moments in his letters when he fulminates in harsh words. There are also moments when he is moved to tears, overcome by sorrow. He was not spared the grief of having to defend his office on occasion. Churches that had first welcomed him with childlike love sometimes dismissed him later at the instigation of false teachers. At moments like these it is not wounded pride that makes him weep, but it is the warm, fatherly compassion for his children that causes him to wince with pain and to grope and search for ways to restore the shaken trust. At times the letters resound with humor, at other times every sentence is filled with jubilation and whole passages rise into hymns of thanksgiving in adoration of the greatness and glory of God. Very often Paul enters into discussion with his opponents. Time and again he interrupts his own discourse with questions that he knows live in the hearts of his readers. Then he stays in conversation with them, chapter after chapter. He reads the questions from their lips, continues from one thought to the next, and then all of a sudden abandons the conversational tone and breaks out ecstatically, ascending to the mountaintops of jubilant faith. He is grateful like a child for every token of affection and deeply moved by a small present given from love. He is not too proud to admit that sometimes on his travels he was filled with great anxiety about a church that did not want to listen to him and that he then yearned fervently for news about them that would console him (see 2 Cor. 7:5–7). Like the old poet of the Psalms, he would lament his loneliness and feeling abandoned, but in the middle of those laments he would suddenly burst out with joy because God had stood by him. Life—all of life, with its many cares and concerns—could at times become a burden for him, so that he began to long for the day when he would be released and be with Christ. Yet this mood never developed into a melancholy pessimism; he always remained standing, conscious with unshakable faith that God, as long as He would leave him on this earth, expected him to offer grateful service to Jesus Christ who gave himself for us. His whole existence was tension and struggle. He once characterized it as "*forgetting what lies behind and straining forward to what lies ahead.*" But in all this tension there remained as an inalienable possession the deepest peace of knowing that "*Christ Jesus has made me his own*" (Phil. 3:12–14). And in his last letters, this peace began to dominate everything, and he could testify with fervid thankfulness that he had fought the good fight and finished the race: "*Henceforth there is laid up for me the crown of righteousness, which the Lord, the righteous Judge, will award to me on that Day*" (2 Tim. 4:8).

When a man like Paul makes the education of the Church his concern, there is no danger of dead rigidity, of intellectualistic reasoning about the truth. Everything in Paul bubbles over with life. Communing with Paul helps you to see that the path of believers is a path they walk with the living God, and that every part of that path is a part of life. Paul's letters traverse the full gamut of human emotions, but in all of them God is present as the deep mystery, a mystery that lifts every emotion to a higher level, to the kingdom of Light, in which Christ is all in all.

7. The Church on the Offensive

A journey of centuries

Centuries have gone by. Paul himself, according to tradition, was beheaded in Rome. The many coworkers who drew their inspiration from him have all passed on. The Christian church in the early centuries did not lose her offensive posture. They blazed a trail in the world of those days because ordinary church members joined the enormous task of proclaiming the gospel to all peoples. Lay missionaries conquered the Roman Empire.

The Church triumphed. She absorbed the idea of a world empire, a legacy of the Roman imperium, and strove to build a new empire, a realm of one religion, one culture, with one comprehensive and binding idea. Beguiled by the dream of that empire, she spread herself in all directions, pitched her tents in distant lands, and toiled at developing the riches with which she was blessed. And the empire arose, the Christian empire, the shadow of the kingdom of God on earth.

But when the dream seemed fulfilled, decline set in as well. Internal abuses sapped the power of the Church, diminishing her moral and spiritual authority. Here and there, fragments broke off the seemingly solid edifice; a spirit of disintegration gnawed at the one, single, carefully achieved Christian culture. Science and learning, timidly at first, began its autonomous work with increasing boldness. Philosophy tore itself free from the embrace of theology and searched for its own potentials. Society developed fresh forms. New problems arose on every side. Trade and commerce brought distant continents within people's horizon. Endless wars for control of the Holy Land led to intensive contact with countries where other ideas obtained, brimming with other cultural ideals. The Renaissance, a revival of the old Greco-Roman culture, held a younger generation in thrall. Humanism awoke, with its confidence in and reliance on the greatness of man and his unlimited ability of mind and hand.

All these new developments generated new problems. Science, it is true, scored brilliant triumphs and opened new prospects, but for all its searching and finding it did not advance the nations toward greater peace and happiness. Skepticism and unbelief laid hold of people, estranged them from all religion, from any belief in an Almighty and Righteous God. Boundless optimism coursed through the world, but sometimes it would suddenly be shouted down by pitiful laments about the meaninglessness of existence and the hopelessness of all human exertion. Wars, which in ferocity and horror surpassed by far anything earlier generations had ever seen, shook the very pillars of civilization and produced a mood of angst and perplexity in ever widening circles. The peoples of Europe became ill, thoroughly ill, because they had lost their inner anchor, because they no longer had the support of belief in a Power that transcends all power of man. Standing in that burning, restless, groping, trembling world stands the Church, the institution that carries the ancient Word, the Word of Him in whom alone deliverance can be found.

If the Church looks back over her journey of many centuries from the point she has now arrived at, she has reason to be ashamed. She has sinned so much; she has been unfaithful in so many things. When unbelief rose up around her like a flood she was often too sluggish even to react; she did not even know how to shut her own gates; she was unable to block unbelief from seeping through her own walls, let alone muster the strength to stand up in that unbelieving, restless world, her arms wide open with compassion about so much misery and so much suffering. Afterwards she woke up from her hallucination and crawled back to the Word; she looked for cover and refuge in the gospel of Jesus Christ; and new life and new strength would stream into her veins and arteries. Yet through it all, something inside her was broken. She became afraid of her own self because she had seen how she had been untrue to her Master. She became afraid for her own children whom she saw growing up amid the temptations of a godless world. She became most afraid of the world itself, of her environment, of science, of the new ideas that roared like a storm wind over the landscape of humanity. And because she was afraid, she could no longer love well. All she could see were adversaries, and she did not see how hollow and empty was the life of those adversaries, and how their seeking and pondering, too, needed the Light of the Saviour of the world.

If the Church looks ahead from her journey of many centuries to the point she has now arrived at, she has reason to be afraid. She sees the rise of powers that may mushroom into a grave threat. She sees opponents looming ahead that will not give her a moment's rest. Dark veils shroud the future. It is as if somber banks of clouds are gathering overhead. And there we stand, armed only with the Word, the same Word that has been our support and our strength throughout the centuries. "That Word above all earthly powers—no thanks to them—abideth." In the grim gravity of these evil times, that Word holds us in its grip, to carry us through the black holes and swirling waters of our distress, onward to a distant future whence will come a new kingdom, the everlasting Kingdom of Christ.

But that same Word which contains such comforting visions, which can speak with a soft and tender voice about the city that needs no light of lamp or sun because the Lord God will be its light, that same Word is also a lash for the despondent and the anxious. It takes us to a high mountain and shows us the world with everything that roils and boils within it, and then urges us to go on the offensive, an offensive from love, from a holy desire to save what is lost. A Church armed with the Word cannot stand idly by, cannot wait till the thunderstorm erupts. She feels herself pushed with iron hands toward the offensive. She must go on the attack, lest she perish. *Attack*—in order that those who live in darkness and the shadow of death will be shown the Light. *Attack*—in order that the wandering sheep that have no shepherd will be shown the Supreme Shepherd and Saviour, our Lord Jesus Christ. More powerfully than ever before, the Church is confronted with the demand to preach the gospel to all creatures. Above the din of world events we hear the trumpet calls that summon us to attack. And then we pick up that same Word in order to find out how to prepare for the attack.

A task for everybody

One of the first lessons we take away from our study is that those who go on the attack should be legion. If the task is left to an appointed missionary over here and another ordained brother over there, the work does not get off the ground. It was a few anonymous lay preachers who swarmed out in all directions that taught the Church of the first century how to attack. This approach did run into difficulties and dangers, but still it was of great value. God used that anonymous work to coax his Church into taking up missions. And Paul, far from monopolizing this spontaneous evangelism, personally stimulated people everywhere and put them to work in order that the campaign could be conducted on an even broader front. He personally assumed a leading role, it is true, and laid a solid foundation, but he had no mind to do the work all by himself. That is an important given that we should turn to our profit. The great war of our time, the spiritual struggle all around us, cannot be waged with a paid professional army. It needs hosts of guerillas, freedom fighters who each do their share to gain the victory.

The Church wages war on many different fronts. She also drops paratroopers onto the mission field overseas, sending lone missionaries far behind the front to launch new beginnings. Of course, no freedom fighters are active there at first. Yet within its own surroundings the proclamation of the gospel must be conducted on a massive scale. Not that it should be done without any order. No, every time again, the guiding hand of the experienced missionary will be needed. During the first phase recorded in the Book of Acts, random proclamation of lay preachers transitioned naturally into the expansion around Paul. The main thing is that every member of the Church knows his place in the attack.

Along what avenues should the attack be carried out? In the Early Church it was done along a variety of avenues. There was in the first place the family, both nuclear and extended. When Paul met a jailer he saw in him his "household": that is, his wife, his children, and his domestic slaves.

Secondly, the expansion occurred along the avenue of societal relationships. The tentmaker Paul met the fellow-tentmaker Aquila and brought him the gospel. A society's various structures offer points of contact, hence also opportunities for preaching the gospel, provided our hearts are constrained by love. When the gospel penetrated the Roman legions, one soldier told another, and so the gospel spread to distant provinces.

In the third place, there is the neighbourhood. People interacted with their neighbours and shared the gospel. Women especially often worked along these lines in the Early Church.

In the fourth place, there is the framework of the nation, the folk, the ethnic group. Wherever a people celebrate its unity—in national demonstrations and patriotic ceremonies, where citizens rub shoulders with fellow citizens—there points of contact are available which can be of great blessing.

Finally, in the fifth place, there is the casual encounter with strangers on the road or in a hotel, meeting with fellow travellers on the same ship or in the same train, coming face to face with prisoners and a prison guard (Paul and Silas in Philippi).

All such occasions, given with the normal make-up of society, can be utilized and made serviceable to proclaiming the Word. Throughout, one inescapable requirement again is that none of us is ashamed of the gospel of Christ and that each of us is filled with the desire to share with others the riches we have received ourselves.

As for the preparatory training of co-workers, the assistant missionaries, what should that training look like? Paul never gave it much thought. He followed the typically non-western way, taking his pupils along on the journey and showing them how things were done. He gave no instructions to Timothy but received him as a companion. After a few months he was not afraid to leave Timothy behind, together with Silas, and put him to work on his own. When Timothy proved unable to resolve a problem and asked Paul for help, Paul helped him, but he also had Timothy stay at his post, no matter how challenging it was for him. At a later date he took this young man back again in his care and had him stay with him for a longer period. On a subsequent journey, Paul sent Timothy all by himself to Corinth, to deal with several pending issues. Timothy failed to restore the peace, so he returned to his master, having achieved nothing. Paul did not become angry with him nor show any disappointment; he simply let his pupil be an observer again for a while so that he could learn from it. Even years later, Timothy often felt that he was not equal to the task, young and inexperienced that he still was; but his mentor stood behind him and backed him up, encouraging, consoling, inspiring, as the occasion required. We are not saying that a course of academic study is superfluous, but we can't help but feel that the best preparation is found in sharing in the work. Juniors join seniors, for the time being mere observers of what happens and how things are done, and before long they are able to pitch in and contribute.

In Paul's days, house churches were important instruments for personal attention and pastoral care. They had something of the intimacy of the home and at the same time of the inclusiveness of the Church. Being a member of a house church made it easy to introduce a neighbour, a casual contact, a close acquaintance, or a colleague from one's place of work. The peaceful atmosphere of the home, where the man of the house steers the conversation, provides opportunities for sharing confidences, answering objections, offering spiritual guidance. The Church of those days needed the house churches because she did not yet own any church buildings and, in many localities, could gather only in private homes. This lack, however, was at the same time her strength. She possessed the instruments to take in the seekers, the half-convinced, and introduce them to the mysteries of the faith.

We need something similar today. Where the threshold to the official church is still too high, where faith formation and catechism instruction is not in popular demand, there homes with open doors must create the opportunities for making contact. House churches in the form of vibrant cells, small circles ruled by fellowship and brotherly love, are the best outposts we can advance for welcoming all those lonely people who are searching and struggling and drifting in our confusing world.

The world then and our world now

That said, we must not forget for a single moment that there is a fundamental difference between the world in which Paul worked and the world in which God has placed us. It is the difference between *not yet* and *no longer*. Paul's world was tired of paganism, was hollowed out and empty, was thirsty for salvation, in whatever form it was offered. People surrendered to the intoxication of mystical ecstasy; they reached out eagerly to anything mysterious, anything obscure; they were ready to accept any teacher and idolize him if he could promise deliverance from the anxiety of existence. They were fascinated by premonitions of a new age; they could glory in a new future; but deep in their hearts was a wound that wouldn't heal; they were consumed by lingering nostalgia and existential angst.

The world in which God has placed us is different. People have experienced the dream of a Christian empire and have seen it fall into ruin. Century after century they have heard the message of the gospel, and they have tuned it out. Life, after all, remained harsh, and reality did not change. People have hated and they have cursed. Deeply discouraged, they have turned away from the Church and from the Word. They have raised their fists against God and shrugged their shoulders at the fairy tale of the Cross. They have turned dull and disillusioned inside. They doubt whether they can ever find a God at whose breast they can sob and weep about the grievous disappointment of all human striving. These are the people we are now to evangelize.

At times, our world is seized by panic, by the madness of looming chaos, by the loss of simple happiness, by the destruction of everything we have built up. At other times, people burst out in raucous laughter, mocking their own fear and fright. They can suddenly be electrified by fresh expectations, craning their necks to see what is rising above the horizon. The next moment, they slump down in despair about paradise lost. Giddy with emotions, they sometimes coast along in their lusts; the very next moment they look with sheer dread at the pain and suffering they have created by their promiscuous passions.

That is the world in which the Church finds herself, holding out her ancient message. As she begins to speak, she runs the risk that people will dismiss her message as old-fashioned and outdated, and they will refuse even to listen to it. As she begins to speak, people will throw in the Church's face her former sins, her cruelty and faithlessness and dissension and self-absorption. In an age of cyclones and tornadoes it's enough to lose all hope as we climb a high mountain and raise our voices to cry unto the cities of Judah: Behold your God! The Church herself runs the risk of defeatism, of moods of despair. Her morale has weakened, her fighting spirit has waned. There are times when the Church would like to rage against the world in furious anger, but then suddenly she stops and wonders whether the world around her is the way it is because of her own fault, because of the Church's lack of compassion and love. Then she is afraid to raise her eyes; then she fears that she will be brutally confronted with her own failures; then her voice breaks.

And all this time, we hear the words of Christ. It is as if we are walking again with Him on a winding mountain path. The horizon broadens, the world expands, our angst grows. "*But you will receive power when the Holy Spirit has come upon you, and you will be my witnesses in Jerusalem and in all Judea and Samaria, and to the end of the earth*" (Acts 1:8). You will receive power, power in obedience, in embracing the calling that God has given us.

How then shall we preach?

And then the question arises in our hearts: How then shall we preach? What are we to say in the world of today, to the people of today? The Word of God speaks about this too.

We have seen how Paul spoke in the world of his time. He was very aware that sometimes he could not begin by saying the things that were nearest to his heart because his audience would not have understood him. He could not mention the Cross first, even though the Cross was the core of his message. He sometimes had to grope for what was best to say first. He sometimes had to wrestle to open the door that blocked the entrance to people's hearts.

There were several things that Paul kept bringing to the fore. In a world still living in the twilight of serving man-made gods, in a world that talked about the God of the philosophers, the universal Logos, the Being of all beings, the Power of all powers—in that world Paul testified first of all to *the living God*, the God with whom we sinful human beings can have a vital relationship through faith. This message unhinges paganism as it were. It overturns all relationships. God lives! He is not a fairy tale, a vague notion, but He is the Creator, the Lord of all things, the Lord also of you. Fellowship with Him is fellowship with a Person, with a divine Thou. It is the fellowship of a child with its Father.

Once the apostle had said these things to his hearers, he could begin to tell them something about the coming judgment. Paganism has no place for a divine judgment of the world; its god is a dead god, a god who is subject to judgment by men who invented him. But once the lines were laid out that lead to faith in the living God, then something could be said, as from a distance, about the coming wrath, and then a deep and rich voice could call people to repent. Following that, the Name could be introduced of Jesus who wants to save us from the coming wrath. That was the message Paul preached to the people of his day.

Now it is not possible, given what we know about Paul's preaching, to draw any one-to-one conclusions as to what ought to be said today. The face of the modern world is too multiform: there are too many diverging currents running through the world today. Besides, God's Word is not a handbook of easy recipes. The one far-reaching conclusion we may draw is that there must be a close rapport between the word that we bring and the audience we are addressing. Not in the sense that we must dress up our message according to the tastes of the audience, but that we must speak to the hearts of our hearers. Of course, in the outward forms we will take their tastes into account, but as to substance the relation is altogether different. And yet there must be rapport. Our preaching must address the questions that live in the hearts; in no way should it slide off people's back and never touch them. It should be concrete and relevant. It should speak to modern man in his contortion and confusion. The Word must never come in hackneyed phrases or outdated diction; it should come at people in a fresh and vibrant way; it has to disturb them in their sterile, comfortable existence; it must cause them to tremble in their need; it must show them that the misery of our world lies much deeper than any poet or thinker has stammered into words, that it lies in the terrible reality we call guilt—our guilt before

God. In short, on the Mars Hills of our day we imagine Paul as Raphael saw him[90]: with outstretched arms, a bounce in his step, compelling eyes, a burning heart. That is how the Church is present in the world, surrounded by the influencers, the champions of knowledge, the world-shapers and world-shakers of our time.

The centuries, like an ever-rolling stream, have come and gone, and the day is approaching when the Church will meet her Lord again. The believers of the first century looked forward to that day with mounting desire, with a longing that filled their hearts and minds. That longing did not make them withdraw, did not turn them away from life's practice. On the contrary, their conviction that the great day was drawing near told them something of God's hurry and haste that is intrinsic to all His works. The world is so big, the nations are so many, the time is so short. The early Christians would pray plaintively: *Come quickly, Lord Jesus,* but even as they prayed the thought would be pressed upon their minds that innumerable people still stumbled along in ignorance. That is why they stayed true to the earth, always abounding in the work of the Lord and always witnessing everywhere, as people who knew that their Lord was coming.

The time in which we live has at least this one thing in common with the time of the apostles: it is a time of deep crisis, of drastic change, the beginning of a new era, a period in which all thoughts and all longings will be turned upside down. In the throes of such a new age, of such a new epoch, we are reminded more clearly than ever that the "King of the ages," the Lord of all, holds in his hands the turbulent history of the world and is leading it to that great hour when the last of the aeons will flow into the Eternal Kingdom. We hear the drone of the engines that are speeding humanity to the consummation of the ages. The apocalyptic visions that John saw on Patmos are closing in on us. It is as if the sum of world history is slowly proceeding to what has been shown us in those visions. As we shudder before all those great events, the Church, moved by the Spirit, cries out: *Come quickly, Lord Jesus!* The Church that waits expectantly, that looks forward eagerly, can never do anything other than be on the offensive. She is quick to preach, to make known the Name of her Lord. She is a waiting church and therefore an attacking church. She is the church militant.

---

[90] [See the cover illustration.]

Even when she is driven back into the catacombs and the bomb shelters, she still attacks.

She attacks. That does not mean she goes out to conquer and destroy, but it means she wins over to life. As long as the Church is on this earth, she will attack. And she will prevail. "*For behold, I am with you always, to the end of the age.*"

Appendix

In Memoriam Dr. H. A. van Andel[91]

by J. H. Bavinck

In recent weeks a flood of news from the Dutch East Indies have arrived in our country, some sad, some happy. It is an unspeakable joy to learn that so many of our missionary workers, about whose fate we have been gravely concerned, have not only survived [the Japanese occupation] but cannot wait to get back to work again. But we have also suffered blows, blows so severe that we will only be able to get over them with great difficulty.

Among those who perished is Dr. H. A. van Andel, for many years a missionary pastor in Solo. As we reflect on the fact that he is no longer with us, we are overcome with profound sorrow. With his passing, missions has suffered a painful loss.

Dr. Van Andel was a man of exceptional ability. A great organizer, scholar, speaker, humorist, a man with an unmistakable talent for practical affairs, highly competent in financial matters, in short, a man of many gifts. In whatever circle he functioned, his word gained immediate authority; in meetings he was a feared debater but at the same time sought after for the wise and powerful leadership that he exuded. But great gifts of mind and insight, however valuable they may be, are ultimately of minor importance when it comes to what a person can accomplish in life. There are far more powerful forces that determine the ultimate result of a life of toil and care. They are especially the willingness to be of service and the dedication to a mighty and magnificent task for which one is willing to make any sacrifice. That Dr. Van Andel was a blessing to countless

---

[91] [Obituary dedicated to the memory of the author's mentor and colleague Huibert Antonie van Andel (1875–1945) with whom for some years Bavinck shared a pastorate in Solo (now Surakarta), the capital city of the eponymous region on central Java. Definitive publication information has been lost; however, judging by internal evidence, the obituary must have appeared in the periodical *Timotheüs*, some time after 22 September 1945.]

many was not in the first place because he was so capable and practical, but because he had put all his strength in the service of a single goal which he pursued above everything else. And that goal was Missions. He was every inch a missionary. Together with his wife, who was his constant support, he would devise new plans, think about fresh approaches, and together with her carry the tremendous work that came to rest on his shoulders.

Van Andel did everything on a large scale. He erected schools, big schools; education had the special love of his heart. He realized the importance of distributing literature, and this too he tackled in a big way. He thought in numbers. Already at the beginning of his work he had set up a scheme for progressive steps in the work he wanted to pursue. Numbers spoke to him; he experienced their seductive charm. Yet for all his love of numbers he was never dry and dull, never just business-like. He was a human being with a most tender heart. I still remember how he once told me that he always composed his sermons deliberately in the form of a rational argument, because he was afraid that he might lose his composure while preaching them. Many a time I have seen him standing on the pulpit, addressing a large audience of young people, when his eyes would fill with tears. The poverty of unbelief and the terrible emptiness of life without God moved him deep in his soul. And that would awaken in him the burning desire to preach the gospel of Christ, to tell it as profoundly and at the same time as simply as only he could tell it.

In his work as pastor he was courageous and strong. He could speak the truth to people and admonish them as few pastors can. There were not a few who sooner or later collided with him, yet I never met anyone who did not in the end come back to him. And no one has ever doubted the sincerity of his intentions. His adroitness at meetings did give him the name sometimes of being too "political," and indeed it was not an easy thing to be his opponent. He had his faults and his temptations, like every human being, but everything about him was in the service of the one great cause to which he had devoted his life.

This would come to light in a sublime way in his practical missionary work, as he stood before highly-placed Javanese leaders. Then he was the man of cultural refinement, fully capable of socializing in circles where the most refined formalities had been cultivated for centuries. Then his whole demeanor was all friendliness and urbanity. But breaking through all that courtesy and friendliness would be the obedience to his Sender, a proud testimony for Jesus Christ, the only Saviour, also of the people of Java. Many cares and disappointments were part of this man's full and active life. He bore them with cheerfulness. God took him in the midst of misery and exile. But the fruits of his labour will remain unto eternal life.

Index of Scripture References

Genesis 2:8 x
2 Kings 5:19 126
Nehemiah 9:6 111
Psalm 104:30 111
Jeremiah 10:10 72
Matthew 21:43 12
Acts 17:30 78
Acts 1:4 4
Acts 1:8 ix
Acts 1:8 139
Acts 1:11 3
Acts 1:15 3
Acts 2:8–11 4
Acts 2:41 4
Acts 3:6 17
Acts 4:18 17
Acts 5:41 17
Acts 6:5 .... 4, 40
Acts 6:7 .... 5, 6
Acts 7 76
Acts 7:2 7
Acts 8:1 5
Acts 8:4 .... 7, 13, 28
Acts 8:9 18
Acts 8:12 17
Acts 9:15 .... 19, 22
Acts 9:19 15
Acts 9:23 22
Acts 9:31 15
Acts 9:32 15
Acts 9:36 15
Acts 10:7 16
Acts 10:9–16 7
Acts 10:24 7
Acts 10:48 7
Acts 11:2 7
Acts 11:3 7
Acts 11:10 18
Acts 11:19 .... 13, 23, 29
Acts 11:20 24
Acts 11:21 18
Acts 11:24 25
Acts 13 26
Acts 13:2 26
Acts 13:3 28
Acts 13:4 28
Acts 13:12 29
Acts 13:16 76
Acts 13:16–42 105
Acts 13:46 33
Acts 13:51 32
Acts 14 77
Acts 14:7 44
Acts 14:15–17 77
Acts 14:16 .... 87, 89
Acts 14:21 45
Acts 14:23 .... 26, 30, 41
Acts 14:26 28
Acts 14:27 .... 8, 118
Acts 15:1–3 118
Acts 15:4 118
Acts 15:10 13
Acts 15:22 34
Acts 15:23 8
Acts 15:36 30
Acts 16:1 39
Acts 16:20 and following. 45
Acts 16:30 15
Acts 16:31 83
Acts 17:1 33
Acts 17:7 46
Acts 17:14 36

Acts 17:16 46
Acts 17:18 86
Acts 17:22–34 .... 81–82, 91–114
Acts 17:30 87
Acts 18:6 33
Acts 18:11 31
Acts 18:12–17 56
Acts 19:9 .... 33, 45
Acts 19:29 35
Acts 19:35–41 124
Acts 19:37 83
Acts 20:4 35
Acts 20:20 .... 83, 86
Acts 20:21 78
Acts 20:31 86
Acts 21:3 15
Acts 21:7 15
Acts 21:8 40
Acts 21:20 8
Acts 22:18–21 22
Acts 24:24–26 84
Acts 26:20 84
Acts 27:3 15
Acts 28:14 15
Acts 28:22 6
Romans 1:16 76
Romans 1:18 and following 122
Romans 3:11 99
1 Corinthians 8 127
1 Corinthians 10 127
Romans 11:15 33
Romans 16:1 125
Romans 16:3 .... 16, 36, 125
Romans 16:4 35
Romans 16:5 120
Romans 16:7 36
Romans 16:9 36
Romans 16:12 125
Romans 16:21 36
1 Corinthians 1:17 86
1 Corinthians 1:19 67
1 Corinthians 1:21 87
1 Corinthians 1:22 86
1 Corinthians 1:23 .... 67, 75
1 Corinthians 1:25 67
1 Corinthians 2:1–2 73
1 Corinthians 2:11 86
1 Corinthians 4:17 36
1 Corinthians 5:2 120
1 Corinthians 10:20 128
1 Corinthians 11:23 24
1 Corinthians 12:2 10
1 Corinthians 15:10 36
1 Corinthians 16:19 120
2 Corinthians 1:19 34
2 Corinthians 5:20 75
2 Corinthians 7 35
2 Corinthians 7:5–7 130
2 Corinthians 8 123
2 Corinthians 8:7–9 123
2 Corinthians 8:19 36
2 Corinthians 8:23 36
2 Corinthians 9 123
2 Corinthians 11:28 34
2 Corinthians 11:32 22
2 Corinthians 12:1–10 24
2 Corinthians 12:1–10. 129
2 Corinthians 12:18 36
Galatians 1:11 67
Galatians 1:17 22
Galatians 2:4 8
Galatians 2:11 8
Galatians 2:13 30
Galatians 2:20 130
Galatians 5:1 12
Galatians 5:2–6 121
Ephesians 5:22–33 122
Ephesians 6:3–8 125
Philippians 2:5–11 128
Philippians 2:25 36
Philippians 3:12–14 130
Philippians 4:3 36
Philippians 4:22 120
Colossians 1:7 36

Colossians 2:2 ... 87
Colossians 4:3 ... 76
Colossians 4:7 ... 36
Colossians 4:10 ... 36
Colossians 4:15 ... 120
2 Thessalonians 3:6 ... 120
2 Thessalonians 3:14 ... 120
1 Timothy 4:12 ... 38
1 Timothy 4:14 ... 35, 39
1 Timothy 5:9 and following ... 125
2 Timothy 1:6 ... 35
2 Timothy 1:11 ... ix
2 Timothy 4:5 ... 40
2 Timothy 4:8 ... 131
2 Timothy 4:9 ... 36
2 Timothy 4:10 ... 35, 37
2 Timothy 4:17 ... 124
Titus 1:5 ... 36, 41
Titus 3:12 ... 35, 36
Philemon 1:1 ... 36
Philemon 1:2 ... 36
Philemon 1:23 ... 36
Philemon 1:24 ... 35, 36
Hebrews 1:3 ... 111
1 Peter 2:18 and following ... 126
1 Peter 5:12 ... 34

Index of Authors Cited

Abbot, L. 68f
Allen, R. 14
Aristotle 49, 52
Augustine 104

Barth, K. 46, 100
Bolt, J. viii
Brouwer, A. M. 39, 55, 105, 120

Calvin, J. 123
Clearchus of Soli 59
Clement of Alexandria 93, 94, 104
Cumont, F. 60

Delleman, Th. 122
Dibelius, M. 98f, 110

Edersheim, A. 54

Friedländer, L. 54

Greenway, R. vii

Hansen, M. 122
Harnack, A. 5, 14, 24, 25, 53, 103
Hoek, J. 60
Homer 47
Holzmann, O. 59
Huizinga, J. 88

Isho'dad of Merv 97, 98

Jones, Stanley 73f
Josephus 9
Justin Martyr 61, 93

Keysser, Chr. 118, 119
Kraemer, H. 58

Lake, Kirsopp 26, 98, 101, 111
Latourette, K. S. 14, 38
Lucius Apuleius 60
Lucius of Cyrene 24
Luke 2f, 6, 13, 18, 24, 25, 26, 28, 31, 35, 44, 45, 46, 76, 77, 80, 84, 85, 86, 113; *et passim*

Mackintosh, H. R. 74
Megasthenes of Soli 59
Minos (son of Zeus) 97

Neubronner van der Tuuk... *see* Tuuk
Norden, E. 59, 95–97, 103, 106

Origen 14, 54, 61

Paul x, 13, 19, 21, *et passim*
Pericles 48
Philostratus 95
Pickett, J. W. 119
Plato 49, 52, 55, 93, 94, 104, 109
Popma, K. J. 60

Reitzenstein, R. 60
Rohde, E. 48
Rutgers, V. H. 123, 125

Schweitzer, A. 99f, 111
Seneca 56, 58
Sillevis Smit, P. A. E. 121

Tacitus 8
Thauren, J. 95
Tuuk, Neubronner van der 105

Verkuyl, J. vii
Visser, P. J. vii

Warneck, G. 95
Warneck, J. 95
Weiss, J. 3, 23, 26f, 97
Wendland, P. 52, 55, 61
Witte, J. 100
Woltjer, R. H. 98, 103

Index of Names

Agrippa (king) ... 84
Alexander the Great ... 49f, 61
Andel, H. A. van ... 143
Apollo (god) ... 78
Apollos ... 35
Apollonius of Tyana ... 96, 106
Aquila, 15, 16, 35, 37, 38, 53, 120, 136
Aratus ... 98
Aristarchus ... 35, 40
Artemas ... 35
Artemis (goddess) ... 45

Barnabas ... 8, 18, 22–30, 44, 77

Celsius ... 14
Cleanthes ... 98
Clearchus of Soli ... 59
Cornelius (centurion) ... 7, 13, 16
Crescens ... 35, 37

Damaris ... 113
Demas ... 35
Demetrius ... 45
Diana (goddess) ... 78, 83
Dionysius the Areopagite ... 113
Drusilla ... 84

Elymas (magician) ... 29
Erastus ... 126

Felix (governor) ... 84

Gaius ... 35, 40
Gallio (governor) ... 56
Gamaliel ... 22

Herclitus ... 93
Hermes (god) ... 44, 77, 78, 87

Isaiah ... 92

Jesus, ix, 1–5, 17, 19, 22, 36, 44, 65, 66, 67, 71, 72, 73, 75, 78, 79, 83, 85, 88, 89, 104, 110, 117, 130, 134, 135, 140, 141, 144
John (apostle) ... 141
John the Baptist ... 84
Jupiter (god) ... 87

Lucius Apaleius ... 60
Lucius of Cyrene ... 24

Mercury (god) ... 87

Nicolaus (deacon) ... 4, 6

Paul ... x, 13, 19, 21, *et passim*
Peter (apostle), 5, 7, 8, 12, 15, 19, 24, 30
Philip (deacon) ... 17, 24, 40
Philip (king of Macedon) ... 49
Philemon ... 125
Phoebe (deaconess) ... 125
Priscilla, 15, 16, 35, 37, 38, 41, 53, 120

Raphael ... vii, 86, 141

Saul ... 19, 21
see also Paul
Sergius Paulus (proconsul) ... 29
Silas ... 34, 36, 136, 137
Simon (magician) ... 18
Socrates ... 93, 94
Stephen (deacon) ... 6

Timothy ... 35–41, 129, 137
Titus ... 35–41, 129
Trophimus ... 35, 38
Tryphaena ... 125
Tryphosa ... 125
Tychicus ... 35, 38
Tyrannus ... 33

Urbanus 35

Wolters, A. viii

Zeno 52f

Zeus (god), 44, 59, 77, 78, 87, 97, 98

Index of Subjects

aides, to Paul.............................. 36–40
Antioch, church of, 8, 15, 18, 24–28, 118
apatheia 64
apostasy:
  Israel's.............................. 7, 12, 129
  pagan 92, 113
Areopagus .... *see* Mars Hill
asceticism 60, 89
astrology 63, 64

baptism 18, 117

cannibalism..................................105n
Christ, 75, 78, 80, 83, 86, 88, 99, 117, 122, 123, 125, 128, 130, 135, 139
  incarnation 79
  crucifixion 12, 74, 88, 139, 139
  resurrection...... 72, 73, 74, 82, 112
  ascension..3
  Second Coming 13, 72, 141
  Judgment Day...74, 82, 84, 88, 140
Christendom......................... 133, 138
Church
  abiding mission 133–142
  legacy 134
  see also congregational life
circumcision.................... 8–13, 18, 32
congregational life
  collections...............................122f
  discipline............................ 119–31
  offices...40f
  ordination 27, 35, 39f
  organization of, 39, 41, 118–23, 129
conscience....................... 55, 120f, 127
conversion, 71f, 84, 110; *see also* repentance
cosmopolitanism....... 50, 51–54, 116

Crusades 133
Cynicism.. 11

deification 60–62, 78
democracy...................................... 48f
deus otiosus...................................... 79

ecstasy 68, 138
elders...30, 129
emperor worship............................ 124
eschatology 3, 11, 71, 73, 82

fasting 26, 28
fatalism 62

gnosticism..96
God-fearers..........7, 15, 19, 33, 44, 76

Hellenism, 50, 53, 55, 56, 57, 62, 63, 112
Hellenists....................4, 5, 6, 7, 17, 24
heresy.. 1
Holy Roman Empire............ 133, 138
Holy Spirit, 4, 12, 25, 26, 27, 28, 30, 32, 39, 89, 113, 114
house churches 16, 120f, 137f
humanism................................54, 133
humanity, concept of........ 52, 64, 109

individualism 55
intellectualism 49, 106, 111, 131
Islam 105n
itinerant preachers. 15, 17, 21–42, 56

Jerusalem Council 8, 13, 22, 25
Jews 30, 32, 58
Judaism.......................... 4–10, 23, 71

Last Judgment 73, 74, 82, 84, 88, 140
legalism.............................12, 13, 120f
letters, 10, 13, 15, 34, 35, 36, 38, 40, 71, 118, 122

see also Pauline Epistles
liberalism 54–56
Logos doctrine 51, 52, 87, 89, 93

Mars Hill 80, 86, 88, 91–124
martyrdom 1
Messiah 11f, 33, 76
metanoia 102, 110
missionaries, roaming 13f, 17, 19, 21–42
missionaries, training of................137
missionary mandate, ... ix, 117, 139
mission field
  ancient 37, 43–67, 71–89, 104f, 115f, 122
  modern 13, 37, 66, 67, 76, 80, 85, 95, 102, 105, 109, 114–20, 122, 136, 138–40
monarchy.................................... 49, 54
monotheism..58
moralism.................................... 56–59
mysticism...................59–64, 106, 111
myths.. 48, 79

nation 8–12, 43, 109, 116, 136
Neoplatonism..............54, 59, 96, 108

paganism, 1, 44, 46, 71–89, 101, 107, 120, *et passim*
pantheism........................... 52, 97, 111
Pauline Epistles, 13, 15, 36, 71, 118, 121, 126, 128, 130; *see also* letters
Pax Romana.......................................63
Pentecost 4, 24
personhood 55
  of God................................108, 140
pharisaism..........................21, 23, 119f
philology.. 95
philosophers...................46, 80, 92, 94
philosophy..........80, 86, 97, 103–110
polytheism.................................... 105f
praeparatio evangelica 104
prayer............. 28, 34, 45, 76, 119, 141
preparatory grace, 54, 67, 94, 104, 105, 106
proselytes....................................4, 8, 76

religion
  Greek 44, 45
  Jewish......................................58, 59
  mystery 11, 60, 96
  national 43, 46, 57
  nature... 58
  pagan......................... 9, 13, 79, 122
  tribal.............................. 43, 52, 109
Renaissance......................................133
repentance, 78, 82, 84, 87f, 101, 102, 103, 110
Roman Empire, 9, 11, 21, 50f, 53, 64, 117, 123
Roman law 11, 123

Sanhedrin 5, 6, 7, 17
science, modern 66, 133f
Second Coming...................3, 72, 151
Septuagint 65, 106
shunning...120
slavery....................... 52, 117, 124, 129
Stoicism 11, 51–67, 81, 91–104
synagogue, 6, 15, 22, 25, 32, 33, 45, 46, 76
syncretism 11, 56–59

technology, modern 66
temple 5, 6, 12, 21f, 25
theokrasia...57f
theosophy...129
translation.......65, 74n, 91n, 105, 111
travel.. 53

universalism..........................48, 50, 58
unbelief...... ix, 67, 115, 133, 134, 144

women, position of...41, 53, 125, 126
worldview, 52, 54, 55, 59, 112, 115, 125

Zion... 12

www.ingramcontent.com/pod-product-compliance
Lightning Source LLC
LaVergne TN
LVHW010703110826
845149LV00014B/3207
9789083661209